I'm Sober, Now What?

Moving through the fear, anxiety, and humility of LIFE, on life's terms.

Willow Green

ADVANCED PRAISE

I'm coming up on my 30th anniversary in recovery and I'm working actively in AA, AlAnon, ACOA-AlAnon and a couple's recovery group. I wish I had been able to read "I'm Sober, Now What" by Willow Green when I was first starting out so many years ago.

For anyone just getting started in recovery I recommend you get a home group, a meeting list, a sponsor, a Big Book, and a copy of "I'm Sober, Now What". These will become priceless tools to get you started, develop a meaningful program of recovery and provide a lifetime of guidance on your "road to happy destiny".

In Recovery,
Gene M.

I have attended many meetings in many countries. I have read many books. I have been in recovery for many years. "I'm Sober, Now What?", by Willow Green is the ultimate guide to recovery. She has brilliantly laid out the tools and how to implement them. This is a must read for anyone that is or has suffered from any kind of addiction. I would even recommend "I'm Sober, Now What?" to people without addiction. The book can help anyone struggling transform their life and find true happiness.

Norm L, Nova Scotia

I've been sober almost four years through hard work, my higher power and the help of Alcoholics Anonymous. AA meetings and fellowship, along with continual work with my sponsor have created the necessary foundation to stay sober a day at a time. The program of AA is fantastic at providing tools and teaching people about the disease of addiction. Willow Green's "*I'm Sober, Now What?*" actually let's people pick up the tools of effective sobriety and shows them how to utilize these tools in their daily lives. This is a must read for anyone in recovery as it application can be applied on a daily basis.

Anonymous, SWFL

Willow Green has taken what might seem to be a daunting task - changing direction and taking control and offered a simple and straight forward approach to self-improvement. Sharing her own journey and sprinkling in stories of others, Willow lays out steps we can use to not only become the best version of ourselves, but to live a joyful and productive life on our own terms. This book is both instructive and thought provoking – well worth reading for anyone who feels stuck or just doesn't feel they are living the life they truly want.

Shelley Simpson

I gift the tools and the knowledge I have gained thus far along my journey to all who choose to use them. May you find the peace and serenity you seek. All you need is within, may you find it now.

So mote it be.

FOREWORD

My journey through sobriety has been much more than just getting clean and sober. This has been an incredible journey of taking back my personal power. When I wrote the first edition of this book, I did not fully understand what that meant. I honestly would have read the words I am typing with a giant ? inside my head. So please know that if you don't understand what your personal power is at this time, it's ok! It means you are reading the right book, please continue.

I wrote this book to myself when I had just gotten sober. I wrote it to the version of me who was lost, confused, and desperately seeking direction. I knew I wanted to heal. I wanted to live. I just did not know how. In the process of writing, I continued to heal, grow and expand.

Among the many things I learned... One of my favorites is that I have a choice. I always have a choice. It doesn't matter what anyone says, thinks, or does. What matters is that I honor myself. I have a choice to follow the crowd and I have a choice to honor my own truth. For many years I followed the crowd. I desperately tried to fit in. I wanted to be liked and understood. Other people's opinion of me was more powerful than my own. I allowed people into my life that hurt me. Why? Because I thought I needed them. I compromised myself, stayed small and handed them my power. I believed that I was going to suffer more without them in my life than the suffering I endured from their treatment of me. I allowed them to play a bigger, more important role in my happiness and my life than I played in my own life. I allowed myself to be controlled by giving into my fear of loss. The only loss I suffered was my personal power and happiness. I gave into my fear, allowing myself to be controlled by others manipulative tactics…I gave away my power in exchange for "perceived" love. I gave away my power in exchange for support. I gave away my power believing somehow I would benefit. I gave away my power believing that these people actually cared about me. I gave away my power by allowing others to invoke guilt and shame, punishing me for my past. I gave away my power trying to prove myself and my worth. I gave away my power begging to be accepted and appreciated. I gave away my power trying to be seen, heard and understood. I gave away my power in exchange for so many false beliefs. All I ever gained from giving away my power was more hopelessness, resentments, and tears. Luckily, as I said in the beginning, I have a choice.

So this second edition is all about me taking back my power. No one is more important in my happiness than me. I have released the toxic people, places and things from my life. I forgave myself and moved forward. I continue to move forward. I continue to release what no longer serves me. I accept myself, all aspects of myself. I honor my needs and thoughts. I love myself and I stay True to my path. I finally love myself enough not to care what anyone else thinks. Your opinion of me is none of my business. I learned that by truly loving myself, by truly accepting myself, and by truly honoring myself…I actually attract more love into my life than I ever imagined possible.

The more I love and honor myself, the more the people around me love and honor me. People treat me the way I treat myself. They learn from what I accept, what I allow and how deeply I honor my own path. The more commitment I show to myself, the more others support that commitment.

While typing this, I was crying with tears of joy and gratitude, because writing this book and actually going through my own process is what leads me to this revolutionary self-discovery and ultimate personal freedom. I invite you to take the journey and find your own path to a healthier, happier version of you! It's worth the effort and the work.

Love,

Willow

CONTENTS

ACKNOWLEDGMENTS

I have so much love and gratitude for the people who taught me unconditional love. Without your support, I am not sure that I would be here and I guarantee this book would not have been written! So thank you from the bottom of my heart and soul to:

The loving memory of Kirk Lusch,

Mom and Don,

Marjorie Fratt,

Susun Weed,

Miki,

Dad and Kathy,

Gordon Cook,

Larry Clapp

The rooms of AA

I love you all and feel so blessed to have you in my life.

1 DEAR MOM

I LOVE YOU!

Dear Mom,

Thank you. I am so grateful for you. Thank you for loving me when I didn't love myself. Thank you for teaching me unconditional love. Thank you for being a beacon of light and love. Thank you for teaching me how to be a rock. You stood strong for the entire family during the passing of both of your parents. You stood strong for me for years. You protected me from everything you could. You stood strong, guiding me. You stood strong, carrying me. You were there for me, even when I didn't deserve it. You believed in me, when I didn't believe in myself. You did everything in your power to save me. You saved me as I slowly tried to kill myself. You pulled me through the depths of my personal hell until I was able to pull myself up. You gave and gave selflessly when I selfishly just took from you. Thank you. Thank you for always giving me your best. Thank you for always doing the best you could to save and protect me. Thank you for being the best mom I could have ever asked for.

I appreciate you. I appreciate everything you have done for me. I appreciated all you continue to do. I am grateful for your support of this book. I am grateful for your time, energy and love editing this book. I showed gratitude and love throughout this book to everyone, but you. Please forgive my inability to show the gratitude and love to you that you deserve. I would not be here without you. I am not sure how to thank you or give back the love you have shown me. I cry when I think of how much I put you through and how much I hurt you. I am sorry. I know those words get overused and mean nothing if the behavior doesn't change. For years, my behavior did not align with my words. They do now. I am present now. I am grateful now. I am the luckiest woman on earth now to have you as my mom. I appreciate you more than I could ever express.

Mom, I will spend the rest of our days making sure you feel my love and gratitude deeper than you felt the pain I caused you. Mom, I love you. Mom, I appreciate you. Mom, I am so grateful for you. You gave me your best for years, and now I am here to give you my best and love you as intensely as you have always loved me.

Love,

Willow

2 DEAR DAD

I LOVE YOU!

Dear Dad,

Thank you. Thank you for being an example of forgiveness. Thank you for being an example of unconditional love. Thank you for loving me when I didn't love myself. Thank you for your patience. Thank you for being an amazing example of how to take the high road. Thank you for teaching me that tough love IS love.

Thank you for saving all the mementos, awards, and special treasures from my past and surprising me with them. Thank you for waiting until I was ready, aware, and able to appreciate you and all you have done for me. Thank you for always accepting and loving me for exactly who I am at that moment. Thank you for teaching me how to be present. Thank you for being the best example of living in the moment. Thank you for being an example of appreciating what you have. Thank you for being an example of gratitude.

Thank you for not pushing me when I couldn't be pushed. Thank you for allowing me to follow my path, learn my lessons, and live my own life. Thank you for respecting and honoring my process, even when it hurt and didn't make sense. Thank you for honoring that I am my own person. I am grateful for your patience, understanding, and unconditional love. Thank you for your willingness and acceptance. It means more to me than words can ever express. I have learned much from our distance. I have learned more from our reconnection. You are an amazing dad. Please forgive the pain I caused you.

I appreciate you. I appreciate you in a way that would not be possible without the pain. My gratitude for you comes from a place that wouldn't exist without your acceptance. I promise to honor you and all you have taught me. I promise to pay it forward. I will spend the rest of my days loving you as deeply and unconditionally as you have always love me.

Love,

Willow

3 INTRODUCTION

FAIL

Fearless And Intense Leadership

-   Willow Green

Once upon a time, not long ago, my life was an unmanageable, chaotic mess. This is not a fairytale; it is my truth. I am sharing my experience, strength and hope. I once heard that by being vulnerable, you give permission to others to be vulnerable. So this is me, being vulnerable. I am sharing my struggles and pain. I am sharing my failures. I am sharing my deepest, weakest, and most embarrassing moments. Why? Because it's my healing process. I have learned that the more I share, the less I hurt.

I carried so much anxiety and fear. Fear that someone might find out what I did. Fear of judgement. Fear of what everyone else may think. Fear of how I will be judged. The fear was crippling. The fear was compounded by the shame, blame and guilt. I was paralyzed with fear over poor decisions. I allowed it to consume me to the point of trying to commit suicide. I had given up. I failed at that too!

Here is my story up to the point of taking 2 bottles of pills and having my stomach pumped. I was a functional alcoholic and drug addict with a deadly eating disorder. I was unable to think clearly. I went through the motions of life, however, I was never actually living. I did what I needed to do to get by. The only thing I cared about was how to get to the next fix. How can I numb myself? How can I make the pain stop? I was miserable. I was lonely in a room full of people. I was a dysfunctional mess. I felt hopeless. I felt scared. I felt so alone, I wanted to die. So I tried.

When I woke up in the hospital, I was so confused. Why was I not dead? Why could I not even kill myself right? The strangest part is when my mom asked me why I lived, my answer was because there would be no one to take care of my dog. I was so attached to the unconditional love of my dog, Doc, his love pulled me through.

I tried to kill myself. I failed. I was miserable and I finally had everyone's attention. I had a choice to make. Life or Death. That was it, I had to choose. I chose life. I asked for help. I went to rehab. I searched for purpose. I searched for God. I searched for answers. I needed a reason to live. I need something, I just didn't know what exactly I was searching for. But I made the choice to move forward in life and give my best effort.

This is where the good part comes, the strength, courage and hope. I not only survived, I thrived. I set out on a journey to save myself. Along my path I have learned so much. I have gained so much knowledge on what works, what is flawed and how to truly let go and love life. I have transformed all of my perceived weaknesses into amazing opportunities to help others. For example, my eating disorder turned into a personal training career. 25 days after I was released from rehab, I started my first day of college. I went to school to figure out how to take care of my new body and my new mindset. What I really gained was a career helping others with body challenges. I graduated school with a 4.0 and went on to own a gym and specialize in working with people with disabilities. I healed myself and helped so many others to heal themselves as well. My eating disorder taught me how to connect with others and show them the way.

Along my path of owning a gym and working mainly in the physical world, I was still exploring more about my life purpose, God, Spirituality, etc. I continued to search for answers. I spent time with many guides and mentors. I asked and was open to all that was being taught to me. I experienced and studied several avenues to find the answers I longed for. I studied Catholicism, Buddhism, Kabbalah, Christianity and much more. I dove into meditation, prayer, manifestations, affirmations, and anything else I could get my hands on. I was open to everything and soaked it up like a sponge. I was willing to receive until the pressure of committing to only that way came up. I could not accept or commit to only one way. That pressure catapulted me down several other paths. It has been an incredible journey of discovery.

I started learning the power of the mind. I started really connecting the dots between mind, body and spirit. The connection finally made sense to me for the first time. I learned how much power I have. I learned to channel that power and energy into manifesting my desires. I learned the impact my thoughts had on my actions and then my reality. I learned that no matter what, if I want my life to change, it begins with me. I am a co-creator of my life. My life is a manifestation of my thoughts. When I changed my thoughts, I changed my life.

So I am here to share how I changed my thoughts, to change my life. I promise you it was not easy; however it has been the most rewarding gift I have ever given myself. We all have the power to create healthy, happy changes in our life.

I invite you on this magical journey with me. Know that any traits or characteristics I recognize is because I have experienced them. My strength and wisdom derive directly from my experience and pain. I no longer see things as good or bad. I see them as experiences. We have two options, learn from them or go through the motions and continue suffering. Pain is inevitable, suffering is a choice.

All names have been changed in this book to protect identities.

4 EXPERIENCE, STREGTH, & HOPE

I walked into a crowded church, heart pumping, terrified as hell and sat in the back of the room. I remember the fear I felt inside. I couldn't speak. I was ashamed, embarrassed, suicidal, and riddled with self-hatred. I just knew everyone was judging me. What were they thinking? Why are they laughing? These people actually look like they are enjoying themselves.

The meeting started. They read some stuff, I had no idea what. They asked if there was anyone who was at a meeting for the first time that wanted to introduce themselves. "Introduce myself?!" I thought. There was no way I was standing up in front of everyone and introducing myself. I was paralyzed with fear.

I listened to the speaker. I have no idea what they said or anything that was said at that meeting. I do remember one thing, at the end they said if you are willing to be a sponsor, please stand. I looked at the people who stood up. The woman next to me stood up, she looked like a yogi and I asked her to sponsor me. It was the hardest thing I ever did. We will call her Jane to protect her anonymity. When I asked Jane to sponsor me, she asked "why now, why are you ready?" My response was simple. "Fear". I explained to Jane that I was living with a man that I feared. I wanted to put a gun to my head to make the pain stop and I wanted to put a gun to his head so that he could never hurt another person. I was terrified of the man I lived with and said "I love you" to. I thought I was going to die and almost welcomed it. This program was my only chance. It was my last option. I was hopeless, broken and had nowhere left to turn. Walking through the fear into that meeting saved my life. All I could think at the time was, "What will people say?"

"What are my parents going to think?"

"People will judge me when they realize I have a problem."

What I didn't realize at the time, was everyone already knew I had a problem. My life was unmanageable. I was out of control. I was depressed. Everyone could see my pain, my fear, my chaos. When I finally told my parents I was going to meetings, they were overjoyed! They were so happy for me. They were proud of me for taking responsibility and asking for help. They were relieved. What I got was overwhelming support from ALL the people who loved me. What I learned was that "I" was the only one who did not know I had a problem. My "hiding" my disease was only wreaking chaos and havoc for those who loved me. My "hiding" and staying in a relationship I feared was only giving that man, we will call Tom, control over me. By me allowing my fear to control me, I gave all my power away. Tom used my shame and guilt to control me. He threatened to expose me and I was his slave. I feared him. I feared for my life.

For the first 90 days, I went to meetings every day. I went to a few different ones until I found the meetings I felt comfortable in. I went daily and at first, this was the only hour of the day I felt safe. This was the one place Tom could not argue with me going to or come and hurt me. I was able to breath for 60 minutes a day. I felt safe for 60 minutes a day. I was with other people who had been through what I was going through. They accepted me without judgement. They welcomed me, hugged me, smiled at me and actually took a genuine interest in my well-being. They let me cry. They listened while I talked. They helped me find solutions to my pain and struggles. They took me to lunch and were kind to me.

They told me they would love me until I loved myself. I cried. I was very confused, broken and hopeless when I walked in, however for the first time, I was feeling hope. I found hope and the will to live and fight for myself.

Here is what I learned that may be helpful to you. Use your own discretion as I can only speak from my own experience. Experience, this is a word I have grown to love, respect, honor, and appreciate. Only someone who has been where I was can truly understand what I was going through. I walked in feeling special, unique and alone. I learned very quickly I was not unique or special. Most importantly I was not alone. What I found was home. I was surrounded by people just like me. I had found my tribe, my community, and my peers. They said, "Keep coming back!" So I did! I was used to people not wanting me to come back; these people actually invited me back. It was amazing. I found a place without judgement. I was accepted, welcomed, and hugged. I was seen. I was heard. My voice mattered. I was able to talk and cry. This was all so foreign to me. Listening to others experience, strength and hope gave me strength and hope. With the support and guidance from my new community, I found the courage and the strength to leave Tom. I learned how to handle situations that once baffled me. I learned where to go when I needed help. I learned all this and so much more.

As the days past, my fear turned into excitement. I looked forward to seeing y new friends, my new family. I was excited to see what I would hear. I grew to a place that I could listen, I could be present. I grew to trust that I would always receive a message. I could go in struggling and it was like everyone knew. Everyone knew what my struggle was and they spoke to me. I felt like everyone was sharing how they overcame that same struggle. I truly felt like the entire meeting was a gift to help me overcome my latest obstacle. It was awesome!!!

Over time, I relaxed. I embraced that the purpose of life is to enjoy the journey. I was so focused on the destination; I didn't know how to enjoy the present. My new family taught me. They helped me learn to feel comfortable in my skin. I learned how to have fun again. I learned to laugh, to dance, and even started to sing again! I started writing again. I found my inner child, nourished her, and set her free.

I have good days and bad days still. I move through painful and challenging situations. The difference is that I no longer do it alone.

I now have a support network. I have tools. I have new

perspectives. I am able to pause, think, and respond appropriately.

Because of this, my relationships have improved. I have healthy,

loving relationships now. I am able to ask for help now. I love

myself now.

The world around me did not change, I changed. Here are some of

the things that I heard that impacted me the most. Many I did not

understand at first. I stayed very open minded. I was hungry for

knowledge, understanding, and a new way of thinking. Over time, as

I did the work, things started making sense.

Addiction promises what recovery delivers.

-Anonymous

Victimization is a form of entitlement. Entitlement and humility cannot occupy

the same space. Humility leads to love, joy and happiness.

-Anonymous

There is no punishment or reward, only consequences.

-Anonymous

The more I learn, the less I actually know.

-*Anonymous*

We have two ears and one mouth for a reason.

-*Anonymous*

The more pain I move through, the less suffering I endure.

-*Anonymous*

Silence allows awareness to emerge.

-*Anonymous*

Acceptance brings peace.

-*Anonymous*

Feel, trust your gut; thinking is what got me into this mess!

-*Anonymous*

Be careful what you ask for, you may get it.

-*Anonymous*

Be aware of your thoughts as they dictate your present.

-Anonymous

Expectations are preformed resentments.

-Anonymous

The best teacher is forever the student.

-Anonymous

Victimization is a form of entitlement; entitlement and humility cannot exist at the same time

-Anonymous

Ignorance- beliefs w/o investigation

-Anonymous

Go where the love is.

-Anonymous

If you spot it, you got it!

-Anonymous

ASK

-Anonymous

You cannot be judged if you do not judge.

-Anonymous

What other people think of you is none of your business.

-Anonymous

We're constantly seeing data. We interpret the data based on our past experience and current reality. The interpretation changes as our knowledge evolves. There is no monopoly on knowledge...I keep changing as my awareness increases. I learn to talk less and listen more

You are in charge of your own recovery. We all have different rock bottoms, triggers, experiences. Pain is inevitable, suffering is a choice. The length of time we choose to suffer is different for each of us. Until the pain of change is less than the pain of staying where we are, we don't change. You are the only one who can decide you are ready. When you commit, life can truly be a blessing full of joy, love and laughter.

5 WHO AM I?

Q-TIP

Quit Taking It Personally

- Anonymous

Imagine your days waking up to the sound of the ocean. As you slowly open your eyes and look around, you see the morning light shining in. You feel well rested, alive and ready to tackle another amazing day. You stretch as you awaken your body before hopping out of bed.

You get up and start the day like every other, by centering yourself. You make a cup of tea and sit outside in the silence. There is nothing but nature, beauty, and you. Your head is clear, you are quiet, calm, and very present.

You enjoy your tea and move into your morning practice of yoga. Your body thanks you as you stretch, strengthen, move and really wake up your joints and muscles. You feel nourished, alive and connected to source. You finish feeling balanced, calm and clear. You are ready to face whatever comes to you today. You are unshakeable.

This is the clarity I worked extremely hard to gain. Moving from restless, sleepless nights of racing thoughts to restful, peaceful nights. It happens when you gain clarity on who you are, what you are doing and why.

One of the greatest gifts you can give yourself is clarity. Clarity of who you are and who you want to be. This does not include the labels you have been given and accepted up to this point. I am talking about the perception you want to have. The amazing person you wish to be without fear, anxiety, or hesitation. The clarity of who you are, your truth. Clarity of why you are here on this earth. Your mission, your purpose and what makes your heart sing. Complete clarity of self. This clarity is not optional if you want to truly be free and live the life you dream of. This clarity is the first step to creating a life more amazing than you dream of.

So let's start there, with who you are right this minute. The more honest you are with yourself, the more you will get out of it. So please take the time to really think about these answers and invest in yourself. You are worth it. Take the time to identify where you are and where you want to go. You may want to print the exercise or write the words on a separate sheet of paper, however I suggest you get a journal to use with this book to keep all your exercises together. It will help you organize your thoughts and allow you to refer back to them.

Start by rating how you feel about each of the following areas of your life, from 1-10. (1) being the furthest from your dream and (10) meaning you are living your dream.

_____ Yourself

_____ Your Body

_____ Your relationship/spouse or lack there of

_____ Your Career

_____ Your health

_____ Your friends

_____ Your co-workers

_____ Your family

_____ Spirit/God

_____ Emotional

_____ Other (please add anything else that may be important to you as well)

- Now that you have identified where you are on a number scale, go back and describe what that means to you. Describe where you feel you are, in detail.

- Next go back and describe where you want to be. Write down in as much detail as possible; what your life looks like in each area when you are able to write down a 10 on your scale.

- Now, look at where you are compared to where you want to

be and identify what's missing. Write down to the best of your ability what you think is missing. Write down what you believe the steps are to get you from where you are, to where you want to go.

What you just identified are your goals. You have created a map of how to achieve your dreams. You have clearly identified what steps you need to take to create the life you dream of. Now that we have clarity on where you want to go, let's clarify who you are.

Take some deep breaths and think of how others see you. Think of how you believe others would describe you. Connect with the characteristics that you feel you portray and that your friends, loved ones, colleagues, etc. would use to describe you. List them. Be honest, there is no wrong answer.

I have included a list of characteristics and their opposition to spark your thought process. Please do not limit yourself to these descriptions, it is only a guide to get you started.

Loving   Vengeful
Accepting   Judgmental/Critical
Gentle   Aggressive/Belligerent
Giving/Sharing   Selfish
Forgiving/Calm   Angry/Anxious

Humble	Arrogant/Controlling
Grateful	Envious/Jealous
Honest	Dishonest/Manipulative
Quite/Tasteful	Loud/Obnoxious
Trustworthy	Sneaky/Suspicious
Forgiving	Resentful/Spiteful/Hateful
Responsible	Irresponsible/Reckless
Open minded	Prejudiced/Defensive
Trusting	Paranoid/Secretive
Considerate/Mindful	Inconsiderate/Rude
Truthful	Fearful/Dishonest
Caring	Abusive
Supportive/Reliable	Unreliable
Cooperative	Competitive
Healthy Boundaries	Enabling
Realistic	Exaggerative/Perfectionist
Optimistic	Pessimistic
Cautions	Reckless
Mindful/Respectful	Disrespectful
Open/Willing	Stubborn/Dismissive
Worthy/Secure	Insecure/Anxious
Honest	Deceitful/Secretive
Unassuming	Conceit

Fabulous job! You are on your way to identifying your qualities at this time. Put the list of your characteristics aside. Now, think of someone that you dislike. Think of what about them triggers you. Write down everything that comes into you mind. Write down all the things that annoy you about that person. If there are others that really get under your skin, feel free to write down those qualities as well. Write down as many as you can that bother you. Connect with all the things you would love to fix in them. Be as honest as you can, no one has to see your list! Refer to the list above if needed for inspiration.

Now, here comes the hard part. Look at each list. Your second list, the one describing who you dislike is YOU. Yes, it is. I know it hurts, but it is your shadow self. When we look at ourselves, the hardest thing to face is our shadow self. Our shadow is the part of us that we do not want to see, we do not want to acknowledge, and we dread. It is the part of us that creates distance between us and the ones we love. Our shadow can be our greatest ally or our darkest enemy. We all have shadows; the difference is how we each express our shadow.

I'm going to share a story about my shadow that may help this sink in a little. One of my biggest shadow personalities is my extreme rage and anger. When I used to get angry, I would scream, punch things, break things and unleash. It was ugly. It was destructive. It was ungraceful. It scared me and everyone around me. I was out of control. I was a loose cannon that allowed my rage to infect everything and everyone I came in contact with. The results were not productive. By the time I calmed down, I was then filled with shame, blame, anxiety, fear and humiliation. I was embarrassed by my behavior and withdrew. How could I possibly face everyone I just punished for something that had nothing to do with them? So it was a very depressing and destructive cycle of anger followed by humiliation. I did not know what to do. My life was unmanageable. Then I found out about shadow work. I learned that the things that trigger me the most are the things I need to change about me. I felt sick. It was the hardest thing I ever had to face. Myself. My demons.

Here's an example from a case study. My clients name is Jennifer; she was not happy. She had a career that she did not enjoy, nor did she make the money she wished she did. This left her feeling emotionally empty and financially frustrated. She moved in with her boyfriend, David, hoping the financial support would relieve that stress from her life. She believed that they could work together and he would be able to support her. She loved him. This was great until their relationship started to go sideways. Neither Jennifer or David were emotionally stable and the stress of living together got the best of them.

Their fighting got out of control. When I asked Jennifer why she doesn't leave, she insisted it was because she loved him. When I encouraged her to get her own place, she always had excuses. When I told her I believed she was staying because she needed the financial support, she became very defensive. This is extremely important. She became defensive at the thought of being accused of needing financial support. This was tapping into her insecurities and her shadow. She would not face the fact that she needed help. Her biggest fear was admitting that she needed David or someone else to help her.

There is no doubt that Jennifer loved David. The problem was that she did not want to admit she needed him. This fear, this secret, this shame caused her so much anxiety. The anxiety and her desire to hide it caused so much destruction in the relationship.

So, the point of that story is this; if you are accused of something and become defensive, there is absolute truth to the words. Find the truth. If I had accused Jennifer of wanting to secretly be a man, she would have laughed at me. If I would have accused her of being a closet lesbian, she would have laughed at me. These things would have not upset her because there was no truth to them for her. So if the words resonate with you, take an honest look at your truth. Until you are willing to see your truth and accept it, nothing will change.

So now the question is how do to deal with it. You need to find a way to nourish that part of you so that it does not come out destructively. Remember my rage? I created a ritual of working out every morning. I start my morning with some form of physical exercise. My favorite is Kundalini Yoga. What this does is allow me to get out all my aggressive energy at the beginning of my day. I feel relaxed, balanced and calm. I have clarity. I release any built up energy. I am able to move through situations with ease. I am training my mind and my body to be able to handle anything. I am training my mind and body that there is a healthy release. I do not need these explosive outbursts to release my rage. I release it consciously and constructively each morning.

Another example of healthy release is from a client named Paul.

Paul has a sneaky, manipulative shadow. He really enjoys being able to deceive people. He nourishes this part of himself by playing poker. Poker is an appropriate outlet for sneaky and manipulative behavior. Quite frankly, it can be extremely profitable if you are good. So your shadow truly can be one of your biggest allies if you choose to embrace it, nourish it and use it to your advantage. Learning to truly love every aspect of ourselves is what leads us to complete freedom and happiness.

Our shadow can sometimes be referred to as character defects. Please do not fall into the rut of believing that you have a defect. You are not defective; you just need a different approach to the situation. Again, we are human and we all experience emotions. We encounter similar situations. We move through life, learning as we go. It's how we handle each experience that defines us. Again, sneaky and manipulative can make you the best poker player, yet the most untrustworthy business person. Same characteristics, different outlet.

Here's another example that may make a little more sense. If your arm hurts, would you cut it off? Of course not! However, this is what you are doing if you believe you can actually remove a "character defect". It is a part of who you are. You are a whole person and on no level should you feel the need to remove a piece of who you are any more than you'd cut off your arm. What you would do, however, is figure out what you are doing to cause your arm to hurt. Then you would STOP doing that! You would use your resources to figure out a new way to accomplish whatever task you were doing without hurting yourself. It is the same thing when talking about your character.

Our shadow self is usually pretty much in line with our so called character defect. So the task is not to remove it, but to turn it into your greatest asset. Again, this is not easy. Nothing that is rewarding is easy. If it were, everyone would do it. Take the time to really look at your list. The next step is to take your "defect" and write down a way to nourish it constructively. The ways in which we nourish ourselves can be by opening ourselves to understanding the opposite, or a healthy release. There is no "one size fits all" answer. You have to figure out what works for you. What makes you feel good inside? What resonates with you? This will show you what you need to work on in order to achieve balance. Here's an example to get you stated:

Shadow Description>>>Opposition to explore or ways to nourish

Allowance	>>>	Set Healthy Boundaries
Rage	>>>	Work out/Breath exercises
Jealousy/Envy	>>>	Practice Gratitude
Arrogance	>>>	Practice Humility/Volunteer
Demand center stage	>>>	Teach/Educate
Lie/Embellish	>>>	Write stories/books
Competitive	>>>	Play sports
Controlling	>>>	Be a personal trainer/Coach
Reactive	>>>	Take 24 hours to respond

These are just a few examples. The key is to truly accept yourself. You have to be able to look in the mirror and accept ALL parts of who you are. You have to love and nourish ALL parts of who you are. If you don't love and accept yourself, why should anyone else? We train others how to treat us by what we accept and allow. Therefore, you have to LOVE YOURSELF before anyone else can or will. We will talk more about that in future chapters.

Let's take a minute to recap who and where you are. You have identified how you feel about your current relationships and feelings in many areas. You have identified where you would like to be in each area and what the steps are needed to achieve it. These steps are your list of goals. So if you have not already, put GOALS at the top of that page.

Through shadow exploration you have identified the areas of your life that need the most attention. This list is what is blocking you from achieving your goals. You have discovered how to overcome those obstacles by nourishing that part of yourself. You know what you need to do to either release the energy or create healthy habits in their place.

You have also made a list of how you believe others see you or how you think you are seen. This list is who you are striving to be. This is the healthy image you desire and can have. These traits will start being your dominant traits as you nourish and release your shadow. The more you can truly understand yourself and who you actually are, the smoother the transition into who you want to be. The man or woman that is free. Free from fear. Free from anxiety. Free, happy, and healthy.

It is now time to release blame, shame, and guilt. These things no longer serve you. You must take responsibility for yourself. This means facing your demons. Taking ownership of your mistakes. Taking ownership of where you are right now. Admitting to yourself exactly who you are, there is no good and bad, just you. Accept and love ALL of you. Take ownership of ALL your actions going forward. Take full responsibility and commit to learning new ways to handle situations. Take responsibility for loving yourself. Take responsibility for nourishing yourself. Make the commitment to yourself, to love yourself enough.

This is your time. You know who you are. You know where you are. You know where you want to go. You have the steps laid out to get there. You know exactly who you want to be and how you want to be seen. You have clarity. You have a guidebook. You have everything you need.

LET'S DO THIS!

6 CALMING THE MIND

KISS

Keep It Simple, Sweetheart

- Anonymous

When Jennifer and David would fight, Jennifer would storm out of the house, slamming the door behind her. She would go for a long walk outside in order to cool off and calm her mind. She always felt better within the first five minutes and could come back with clarity to assess the situation. Other times, David would follow her. He had extreme abandonment issues that paralyzed him with fear. He thought if Jennifer left, she would never come back. In his mind, she was leaving him. He could not comprehend that she was actually choosing not to react, but to go calm down and clear her mind.

Jennifer knew that when she was angry, she couldn't think straight. She was going for a walk in attempt to defuse the situation. When David followed her and continued the argument, it usually got very destructive. His fear only caused more pain for both himself and Jennifer. His inability to allow her the time and space she needed to cool off only created more rage inside her. He followed her and verbally attacked her until she eventually broke. She was so empty, defeated and exhausted she gave up. She eventually left him for this reason. David's need to have answers and inability to allow her to calm down lead to the destruction of each of them and their relationship.

When David was alone, feeling abandoned, he was forced to look in the mirror. It took about a year, however he finally learned that Jennifer's walks were her attempt to stop the fighting and save the relationship. He learned about calming the mind. He learned that there would be no constructive communication until he could calm down and speak clearly. He learned that in the heat of the moment, when he was not thinking clearly, he was not able to rationalize his behavior either. His crippling fear of abandonment was what actually lead to what he perceived as abandonment.

When he finally gave up blaming and attacking Jennifer and looked at his part in what happened, an amazing thing happened. He recognized the importance of pausing when things get heated, and calming the mind. He learned how to calm himself and began enjoying the experience of being able to think clearly and rationally. This was not at all an easy process for David, however, with commitment and dedication, he did it. He is now able to take a deep breath, pause, calm himself and look at the situation with a new perspective and sense of clarity.

David now has a new sense of self-worth, his business relationships have improved, all of his relationships have improved. His life is much more rewarding and peaceful. He has learned how to control his reactions rather than allow his circumstances to control him. He has even repaired his relationship with Jennifer and learned to honor and respect her time and space.

This process was the hardest thing David ever did, and also the most rewarding. He implemented several tools and worked on himself until they became his new habits. It took David time and effort. The biggest thing he realized was that the change wouldn't happen overnight. It took commitment and consistent effort. He had to embrace the fact that behavioral change is a process, not an event. It evolves slowly over time until it becomes second nature.

During David's year of consistent effort in calming and clearing his mindset, he noticed several other benefits as well. Here are just a few of the other things that he experienced:

- Improved ability to sleep
- Reduced stress and anxiety
- Reduced headaches and tension
- Increased blood flow
- Reduced inflammation
- Increased happiness

- Increased mental clarity
- Increased ability to control his emotions
- Increased energy
- Decreased explosive reactions
- Increased ability to be present and enjoy the moment, enjoy life

What did David actually do to achieve this and how can you? How was he able to clear and calm his mind? He used several techniques. There are so many out there, we are only going to cover a few. The key is to find the tools that resonate and feel comfortable to you. If it works, keep it. If it doesn't, try a different approach. Whatever you do, don't give up. Keep trying until you find what works for you.

Breathing is the first tool I am going to discuss. It seems so simple, yet it is not. Pay attention to your breathing right now. I would be willing to bet it is shallow and you are taking several breaths per minute. What I would like you to try is long, deep belly breaths. The easiest way to learn this is to lie on your back and put your hand on your belly below the navel area. Now take a deep breath in through your nose, breathing deep into your belly, enough to lift your hand. Practice slowing your breathing down and connecting to your breath. Count to 10 as you inhale and then count to 10 again as you exhale. Do this at least 10 times. If you need help, please Click here and schedule a FREE discovery call with me. You will notice as your breath slows and regulates, your mind slows and clears. Any racing thoughts will slowly fade away.

Regular practice will remind you that you have the ability to breath anytime, anywhere. The more you connect to the breath, the less reactive you become. You increase your ability to think clearly and handle any situation with clarity.

Another trick when you need to change your energy is to practice different nostril breathing techniques. Breathing through only one nostril at a time can completely change your energy. For anxiety, plug your right nostril and take 26 long, deep breaths through your left nostril. This should calm you. It is also a great exercise when you can't sleep at night. If you are feeling sluggish and tired plug your left nostril and take 26 long deep breaths through your right nostril. This should revitalize you and give you energy.

Another great way to change your energy is to ground yourself. The best way to ground yourself is to walk around outside barefoot. If you do this regularly, you will notice multiple beneficial results, many of which were David's, listed previously. When you connect to the earth, you exchange ions. Without going into the science of it all, know that as you connect with the earth, you are stabilizing your body systems. You are releasing anxious energy into the earth while simultaneously pulling the energy you need for clarity into your body. Take 5 minutes to go outside and try it!

Have you heard the expression "tree huggers"? I bet you have! There is more to hugging trees than just being a hippie. This too is another way to ground yourself and release crazy energy if you need to. If there is no tree, just put your hands on the earth, preferably in the grass or dirt. Close your eyes, take a deep breath and ask the tree or earth to exchange energy with you. There is an abundance of unlimited energy coming from the earth. You are not hurting the trees or any other part of nature through the exchange, there is plenty of energy for everyone. It may sound strange, but I challenge you to give it a try. These are simple ways to clear your mind quickly and easily. The quicker you can regain control of your thoughts and gain clarity, the quicker you can move toward a healthy solution.

Breathing and grounding are ways to immediately change your energy and clear your head. Creating a daily routine or practice including some form of yoga or exercise will increase your ability to handle the situations as they arise. The daily practice is like samuri training. You must prepare yourself to handle anything.

Pick something and commit to it for at least 30 days. Put up a calendar and cross off each day as you finish your practice. Whatever you choose is fine. It can be as simple as walking for 10 minutes a day to clear your head. The goal here is not what you commit to, but that you actually commit and accomplish what you have chosen to do. You need to do this to train your brain. Train yourself to push through on the days you don't feel like it. Train yourself to MAKE the time to clear your head. This may be a challenge in the beginning, but it will turn into the time you cherish the most. You are setting yourself up for success. You are setting yourself up with the tools to clear your mind. You are teaching yourself how to become calm and clear. As your destructive reactions decrease and your clarity is formed, life becomes much more pleasant and calm.

When your mind is calm and you can evaluate a situation with clarity, you achieve the results you want. You have the power to handle the situation with dignity and grace. Your clarity allows you to move through anything. You can start to evaluate rather than react.

With clarity, when you feel blind-sided, you have the ability to sit back and ask yourself some very important questions. These are some powerful questions to help you work through anything life throws your way:

- Is this situation real?

- Or is this in my head?

- What is really going on?

- What is the real reason I am upset?

- Is it about this or has something triggered from my past?

- Am I hungry? Angry? Lonely? Tired?

- Do I have all the information?

- Does this need to be said?

- Does it need to be said by me?

- Does it need to be said now?

- What is the worst thing that can happen? Can I live with that?

- Is it possible that I misunderstood?

- Is there another way?

- Is it more important to be right or to be happy?

- Am I blowing this out of proportion?

- What would happen if I pause and come back to this?

- Is there someone I can talk with in order to gain more clarity?

- Am I reacting out of fear?

- What am I afraid of?

- Who am I afraid of?

- Why does this scare me?

- Am I being honest with myself?

- What is my intent?

- Am I responding from a place of integrity?

Take the time to really work on your breathing, grounding and 30 day challenge of choice. It is impossible to move through any situation productively without clarity. You have put so much effort into gaining clarity of who you are and where you want to go. You have mapped out the steps to achieve your dreams. Now you need to be able to calm you mind and stay focused on your goals. The faster you can calm yourself, the easier it will be to stay focused.

7 NOURISHING YOURSELF

FINE

Frustrated, Insecure, Neurotic, Emotional

- Anonymous

Think back to when you were a kid. Remember when you had something really exciting about to happen? A family vacation. Field day. A slumber party. A trip to the amusement park. You know, something that you were so excited for you couldn't sleep at night. You tossed and turned with anticipation. You rolled over checking the clock. Then you tried to go back to sleep, it felt like an eternity. You rolled over to check the clock again, thinking it must have been at least an hour! Only to find out it has only been 2 minutes since the last time you checked!

Finally, after hours of tossing and turning you manage to finally fall asleep 5 minutes before your alarm actually goes off, if you managed to sleep at all. Despite your lack of sleep, you leap out of bed. You aren't at all tired. You have all the energy in the world as you get ready for your day of great adventure. Nothing is going to stop you.

This is the part of you that we need to find again. What is it you crave? What experiences are you longing for? What are you passionate about? What are you doing when you completely lose track of time? What are you daydreaming about when time seems to stop? Where do you go when you zone out? What are you thinking about?

If you are not sure what you are passionate about anymore, ask yourself;

If I had all the money in the world, unlimited resources and could do anything, what would I do? What would I be so excited about to jump out of bed and do in the morning?

The number one answer I hear is "I would travel". I think traveling the world would be exciting, absolutely. However, would it truly be as fulfilling as you think, just traveling? What would you do when you get there? What would be the purpose of your travel? Would it be to go build wells in third world countries? Would it be to explore art and culture? What would you be traveling to and why? What are you seeking? What do you hope to gain from the experience? What is it you are really after?

Really dig into those questions. As you start to gain clarity on what you are truly seeking, it will unravel a road map of how to get there. If you seek art and culture, what can you do today to seek art and culture locally? How can you open up your mind and your life to allow that part of you to evolve naturally? What local groups can you join to learn and grow toward that area you seek?

Take the time to invest in what you want your life to look like. Take your journal and find a quiet place where you will not be interrupted. Take a few deep breaths and connect to yourself. Ask yourself, what does my dream life look like? Then write it out. This is your dream and there are no limitations, no one is watching, no one is judging. You are all that matters. Write out exactly what you want your life to look like. Write in as much detail as possible. Write about your ideal career, your lover, your travel, your family. Write down in detail where you want to live, how you want to feel, about your relationships with others, your relationship to yourself. Write about how you want to be seen, how you project yourself to the world. Write down everything that you want in your life. Write down everything, even if you think it's too big or impossible. Write it anyway. No limits. The only limits are your mind. Connect to your dreams and let them flow. Write it all.

WOW! How awesome was that? How are you feeling right now? I hope amazing. Connect with that feeling, the feeling of having everything you just wrote down. Imagine yourself living that life. See yourself living that life. Feel yourself living that life. Remember this feeling.

This is what motivates you. This life is what you should be working toward. Every decision you make should reflect what you dream of. Ask yourself, "Is what I'm doing leading me closer to this life? Or further away from this life?" Then decide if what you are doing is worth it.

This is the overall goal. There has to be many little victories along the way. Little ways to allow yourself to feel amazing, nourished and in love with yourself.

What will help you stay on track? What little things make you feel good? Is it your morning meditation? Yoga? A long walk? A trip to the gym? What keeps you on track? What helps you stay connected to your long term goal?

If you are feeling lost, are you willing to ask for help? Are you willing to be vulnerable and ask for help? For a long time, I wasn't. My inability to show what I perceived as weakness kept me stuck. My inability to feel worthy of help kept me stuck. My messed up thoughts kept me stuck. I unstuck myself by moving. I unstuck myself by being willing to move out of my comfort zone. I unstuck myself by taking chances. I unstuck myself by loving myself enough.

Here is what I mean by all that. I love pedicures. For a long time, I chose not to get them. Not because I didn't want them, but because I didn't feel worthy. I owed people money, I had bills, I had so many other things that I felt deserved the money and attention more than myself. So I put the money toward that and neglected myself. What ultimately would happen is the energy inside me would fester and build. Why was I not good enough? Why didn't I deserve a pedicure? This all sounds ridiculous, right?! Here's the thing, when I just went and got the pedicure, I felt amazing. Up until that point, my mind was consumed with what I thought I deserved or didn't deserve. What really mattered is what do I need to do to move through this crazy energy I felt. I needed to just go indulge, nourish myself for that hour and refresh. When I did, my mind was clear. I felt beautiful and amazing. I would often think to myself, what the heck took you so long? Why did I waste so much time and energy fighting with myself? Time and energy that could have been used on something productive.

Do you see the point? It's not about what you can or can't do. It's about what you decide to do. It's about what makes you feel good. When you feel good, everything is easier. When you feel good, your thoughts are clear and you see things in a new perspective. When I was punishing myself by not taking care of myself, I was angry at others. I would see other people taking care of themselves and get pissed. My mind would take me to unhealthy places, thinking why can't I have that? Why do they get to feel good and I don't? What makes them so much better than me. I was angry and looked at other people like they were more deserving. But why? The only reason was it was all in my head. They were not better than me. I was the only one holding me back. I was in a place of unworthiness. No one put me there, no one was holding me there. Only me. I had the power to get out. When I used my power to get out, my entire reality changed.

After getting my pedicure, I felt beautiful. I felt nourished. I felt like a princess. I took care of my needs. I didn't need anyone else to do it for me. I knew what I needed and I took care of it.

The same goes for when I need a massage. I don't sit and complain or feel unworthy. I do what I need to do for me. It is my responsibility to listen to my needs and take care of them.

When I am feeling anxious, I rollerblade. When I feel stuck, I move, I walk. When I am in my head and cannot get out, I call a friend. There is always a solution if we really want one. If you are stuck, use the exercises from the last chapter, calm your mind and ask yourself, what is it I really need right now to move through this? Then open up and listen to the answer.

The more you can understand your needs and nourish yourself, the healthier all of your relationships will become. We learn to love ourselves. Then we teach others to treat us by how we treat ourselves.

Another example is sports. If you love playing soccer, basketball, softball, join a team. If this is a part of your childhood you cherished, then find a way to cherish it as an adult. Not only will you be able to enjoy the sport, but you will also connect to a new group of people. As you nourish the parts of you that are missing, you align yourself with a new network of people. People that are in sync with you and your goals. You broaden your mind. You open up to new ways of thinking and doing. You attract the joy as you enjoy. You start to feel again. You start to laugh again. You are part of something much bigger than just yourself.

If something feels good, move toward it. If something hurts or feels painful, stop doing it. Listen to what your feelings are telling you. Nourish the parts of yourself that need nourishment. Nourish them without fear, guilt or shame. Love yourself enough to enjoy what you wish to enjoy. Move through the discomfort of trying something new so you can experience the joy of following your heart. You are the only one who truly knows what you need. No one else can do this for you. Own your life. Nourish yourself to joy.

8 CLEARING THE EXCESS CRAZINESS

RELEASE

Real Empowered Love Enables A Safe Exit

- Willow Green

Congratulations! Please give yourself a pat on the back for all the work you have done. I am so proud of you. You are so far along your path to successfully living your dream. You have clarity of who you are. You know exactly where you want to go. You have all the steps plotted out on how to get there. You have taken complete responsibility for your future and your happiness. You are on your way to mastering your ability to slow down, breath and clear your mind. You know what motivates and nourishes you. You know what your dreams are. You have written down exactly the life you are creating. You know that your actions are taking you toward your goal. You are taking control of nourishing yourself and you are feeling amazing.

The next step is clearing out what no longer serves you. I like to call it clearing the excess craziness! What is stopping you from doing what you need to do? What seems to be getting in the way? You know what you need to do to take care of yourself and your needs. Who or what is a distraction? Who or what are you giving your energy to instead of focusing it on what you need to do?

Make a list of everything you do in a week. Include what you are currently doing as well as what you wish to add. For example, if you decided to join an athletic team, but are struggling to find the time, include it. Include your responsibilities as well as needs and wants. Write down everything. This should be easy since you just figured out your needs in the last chapter.

Here are some examples:

Work

Yoga

Gym

Game night with friends

Meditation

Dinner with family

Take kids to school

Music lessons

Movie night

Read

Study

Be of Service/Volunteer

Free time

Dance lessons

Date night

Personal growth time

Travel

Alone time

Work in the garden

Now look at your list. Is there anything that no longer serves you? What on that list does not align with your dream? What on that list does not feel good to you? What can be eliminated? If you can eliminate something that no longer serves you, do it. If something doesn't feel good, but you cannot eliminate it yet, we will work through that.

Cross off whatever you can eliminate at this time. Then rewrite the list in order of what is most important to you. Understand, this is the order of what feels the best to you, not what you think should be important. For instance, your job doesn't have to be number one just because you need money to survive or to support your family. Put everything in the order that aligns with helping you feel amazing.

Here is an example:

Most important to least important

1.   Yoga

2.   Laughing

3.   Connecting with nature

4.   Reading/Personal Growth

5.   Writing/Painting/Creating

6.   Enjoying Friends

7.   Trying new experiences

8.   Working with Clients

9.   Returning emails/phone calls

10.   Marketing and Computer Stuff

This is my list. These are my must haves in the order that they feel good to me. This doesn't mean that number 10 is any less important than number 1. It means that this is the order that feels good to me. I wake up every morning and I start my day with Yoga. It clears my mind, releases all energy that no longer serves me and gets me into the mindset I need to tackle the day. It is what I do for myself to ensure I am present for my clients. If I am worried about anything or thinking about anything other than my clients when I work with them, I am not serving them. I take care of me, so that I can be of maximum service. When my head is clear, I can completely focus on what they are going through. I can see their situation and help them move through it with clarity. I can be there fully for them without my thoughts or my life getting in the way. I am 100% in a solution based place for the person I am giving my attention to.

So how can you be 100% present. By setting yourself up for success. Let's map out your weekly schedule and create your success with even more clarity and detail. This is an example of my schedule right now. Use this as a guide to write out your week.

	Sun	Mon	Tues	Wed	Thur	Fri	Sat
8-9	<<<<< YOGA / Meditation >>>>>>>>
9-10	---------- >>>review emails<<<< ------
10-11	----- >Clients< AA Meeting >clients<----------
11-4	---- >Clients<Networking>Clients<Fun w/ Friends
4 - 6	--- >>>> Clients<< Networking >>> Clients<< Fun!
6 – 8	AA >>> Nature <<< Reiki Circle/ Kirtan/Community

Perfect! Now look at your schedule. Notice any patterns? What you are doing is teaching your brain to focus on what needs to be done. You are teaching yourself to see what you need to do to move toward your dream life. Is your schedule in alignment with your steps toward your goal? If so, fabulous. If not, what needs to change? What needs to be eliminated? What needs to be added? Take the time to figure this out. In order to reach your dream life, you must align your day to day activities.

At the beginning of this chapter, I asked you who or what was getting in the way. I asked you where your energy was going when it wasn't going toward your goals. I need you to look at the answers to those questions. What do you need to do to eliminate that distraction?

I was working with Sue. Sue is a very loving mother that put so much energy into her children. Her life revolved around her children. She took little time for herself and even when she did, she was constantly interrupted. When she finally called me, she was depressed, exhausted and had lost all sense of self. She was tired and snapping at the kids all the time. She couldn't figure out what was wrong and why she was angry all the time.

When I asked Sue what she does for herself, she looked at me confused. Her day consisted of getting the kids up, making breakfast and getting them off to school. While the kids were at school, Sue did laundry, cleaned the house, did the shopping and tended to whatever other needs her kids or husband needed. The kids got home, she helped with homework, made dinner, cleaned up, got them ready for bed and put them to bed. By this time, Sue was exhausted. However, she then would spend time with her husband, whom she loved, and he also wanted her attention and affection.

Sue was extremely loving, yet increasingly angry. She started snapping at her husband and the children. She felt horrible and did not understand where this came from.

I asked Sue what would make her happy, something that had nothing to do with her family. What could she do to love herself as much as she loved them? She was unsure. So we started with having her create a sacred space that was hers and hers alone. This was her personal mesa. I asked her to go to her personal mesa every day for

5 minutes. I asked her to train herself that this was her safe place. This was a place for Sue to let go. She was instructed to go to this place when she could be uninterrupted and sit in silence. I asked her to connect with what she feels and learns in this space.

Sue returned for the following appointment with less anger and a twinkle in her eyes. What Sue learned was that taking time for her was exactly what she needed. She began bringing things into the space that made her happy; candles, scarves, crystals, pictures, etc. Sue had created a safe, personal space that brought her joy and peace. As time went on, when she was feeling angry, she would return to her mesa to clear her mind.

Sue also trained her family. She recognized that when she was able to step away from the situation and clear her mind, she was able to return to her loving place. She was not only helping herself, but also being the best mom and wife possible. So she explained to her family what her needs where. She asked that when she is in her mesa, they do not disturb her. Sue set the boundaries she needed to take care of herself. Her family quickly saw the change in her. They realized that her boundaries are out of love. They did not enjoy her anger any more than she did. Allowing her to go sit in quiet for whatever length of time needed, allowed Sue to come back refreshed and nourished. When she was refreshed and nourished, the entire family benefitted from her love.

What I hope you learned from Sue is that boundaries are for everyone's benefits. As you take care of yourself, everyone benefits.

The more you love and nurture yourself, the more you can love and nurture the ones you love. You have to start with yourself. It's like being on an airplane, put your mask on first. If you pass out, you cannot help anyone. Save yourself and you are of maximum service to everyone.

9 NEW PERSPECTIVE

"Everything we hear is an opinion, not a fact. Everything we see is a perspective, not a truth."

- Marcus Aurelis

Imagine yourself in a glass box. See the box all around you, right, left, front, back, above and below. See the glass as thick and sturdy, about 1 inch thick. It is unbreakable, shatter proof glass. Imagine yourself in the center of the box. Now see a hole, about the size of a quarter. Think about where in the box this hole is. Stare at the hole. See smoke coming in through the hole and filling your box. The smoke is coming in quicker and quicker. Your box is filling up. You realize that this smoke is heavy and thick, if your box completely fills up, you will pass out. You must get out quickly to survive. You have no tools. You cannot break the glass. You cannot get out through the hole. You must get out, now. How do you get out? What are you going to do?

If you have not figured out how to get out of the box and need help, please email me and schedule a FREE discovery call for answers.

How did that feel? Were you able to get out of the box without looking at the answer? Did you start to feel claustrophobic? Did you start to panic? Was the answer obvious to you? Think about the emotions you felt. Depending on how your mind works, you either felt this was an enjoyable experience or a terrifying one. It's all about your perspective of the situation. Life is very much the same way. It's all about your perspective. How you choose to see each situation.

One of the biggest arguments is whether the glass is half empty or half full. People debate which way to see the glass and who is right and why their view is better. Personally I think that is a waste of time all together. Sometimes I see the glass as half empty, other times I see it as half full. The way I see it depends on the mood I am in that day. It depends on what else is going on that led up to the point of deciding how I see the glass. It really doesn't matter how I see it. I see it, I acknowledge it and I move on.

Let's do a visual to help you understand. Go get a glass and fill it half way with water. Now hold it in your right hand about shoulder height. Look at the glass. Ask anyone who is around if it is half full or half empty. Continue to hold the glass for at least one minute. One minute doesn't sound like much, however if you are doing the exercise, then I bet your arm and shoulder are starting to burn a little. Hold it for five minutes and you will really feel a burn. Hold it for ten minutes and you will start to go numb if you can manage to hold it that long. Are you starting to get the point? It doesn't matter how you see it. It doesn't matter how anyone else sees it. Agree to disagree and set the glass down. The longer you hold on to something the more painful it becomes. Just make a decision of how you wish to view it, own your decision and move on.

The more time you waste bickering over who is right, the more pain you cause yourself. The more energy you put into trying to get someone else to see what you see, the less energy you have for something meaningful and productive. Agree to disagree and move on to the next thing. It seems so simple, yet it can be so difficult to just let go, not worry about who is right or wrong. Honestly, no one is right or wrong. We all see through our own eyes and our own experiences. No two people will ever see the same thing.

My best friend and I experiment with this phenomenon. We completely understand that we see the world very differently. We do not argue about who is right. We choose to respect each other's opinion and make a game out of it. We sit and stare at the same thing. She describes what she sees, in as much detail as possible. I then describe what I see in as much detail as possible. We see different colors, shapes, etc. We choose to learn from each other. I find her view fascinating.

We interpret life through the language we learn. We learn from our experiences, the people who raised us, and the teachers we have met along the way. We then communicate in the only way we know how. Different cultures speak differently. They are all saying the same thing, only with different words. Think of every person you encounter as being from a different culture. Would you have more patience? Would you make more of an effort to understand what they are trying to say? How would you communicate with them differently? Take mom, dad, lover, someone close to you for example, how would things be different if you had more patience? How would your relationship be different if you were more open minded and tried to understand her perspective? On the same note, how would you feel if when you communicated, people took the time to ask you more questions? How would it feel to have someone make an effort to understand you rather than jump to conclusions? How would it feel to have someone take the time to hear you and understand your perspective? I bet it would feel amazing!

This leads me to the Golden Rule, as defined by a Merriam Webster dictionary: "A general rule for how to behave that says that you should treat people the way you would like other people to treat you." We are all very different people with different needs, wants, desires, etc. We all have our own rhythms that feel good to us. Try getting to know each person as an individual. Take the time to learn their likes, dislikes, needs, wants, triggers, quirks, etc. By investing in this discovery, you set yourself up for a positive, healthy, rewarding, reciprocal relationship.

Examine this example of Doug and Sara on their first date. Doug had a crush on Sara and finally got up the nerve to ask her out. He wanted to impress her, so he planned the entire night. He loved Indian food, so he took her to his favorite Indian restaurant. Sara was not familiar with Indian cuisine. Doug told Sara all the things he loved and ordered his favorite appetizer. He told her what his favorite dishes were and said she would love them. He went ahead and ordered them, telling her to trust him. When the food came, Sara about gagged. The appetizer was heavy and meaty. All the dishes were heavy and meaty. Sara was a vegetarian with a sensitive stomach. Needless to say, there was never a second date. Had Doug taken the time to learn about Sara at all, he may have made different choices, involved her in the decisions, and maybe had a second date!

More on perspectives. Think about judgment. Did you know that you cannot be judged if you do not judge? Here's what I mean, if you have body issues, you constantly judge bodies. If you feel you are imperfect, you notice everyone else's imperfections. If you love your body and have no body issues, you don't notice other people's bodies, it doesn't faze you. The same goes for hair, make-up, clothing, etc. We only see in others what we are critical about ourselves. So if you learn to accept yourself and love yourself, you will see only love and acceptance. If you notice yourself continually judging others, ask yourself why you do not love yourself. These are the best opportunities to change our view from others to self-reflection. Everything is a reflection of what we dislike about ourselves.

When you get stuck, here are some ways to force yourself into a new perspective:

- Where is this really coming from?
- How would it look if I remove attachment to the result?
- Am I Hungry, Angry, Lonely or Tired? Could this be clouding

my thoughts?

- Why is this bothering me so much?

- What is this situation reminding me of?

- Who is this person reminding me of?

- What am I feeling? Powerless? Hopeless? Anxious? Envious? Jealous? Fearful?

- What is the worst thing that can happen?

Sometimes you can explore these questions immediately and change your perspective, other times you may be clueless. If you are clueless, write down what happened in as much detail as you can. Keep a journal handy or jot it down in your notepad in your phone. Doesn't matter where, just get it written down. Put down the circumstances, people involved, how you are feeling, what emotions are being brought up, etc. The more detail the better, so you accurately analyze the situation later.

Now, make time to reflect. Go sit by your mesa (or a sacred place to you), clear and calm you mind, and know you are in a safe place to explore what you were experiencing. When you are clear, calm and ready, review your notes. Ask yourself;

- What is the root of my discomfort?

- How can I see this situation differently?

- How could I handle this situation differently?

- What can I learn from my emotions?

- What part did I have in this discomfort?

- Show me what I need to know?
- Or ask whatever questions feel right to you….

Then sit still and listen. Be patient and allow the answer to flow into your thoughts. Do not judge yourself. This is an exercise that when performed with an open mind can help you gain more clarity on the experiences you have, and why.

The biggest challenge is to detach yourself from labeling the experience "good" or "bad". Instead, accept that each experience is just that, an experience. If we enjoy the experience, fabulous! If we don't, fabulous! What you have gained is self-awareness and clarity. If you enjoy an experience, do more things that lead to similar, enjoyable experiences. If you did not enjoy the experience, learn what you did that led you to that experience and don't do it again. It seems really simple, because it is really that simple.

Do what leads you to the things you enjoy and stop doing things that lead to things you don't enjoy!

A great way to recognize when you are moving toward things that don't feel good is to start recognizing resistance. Resistance comes in so many forms.

Here are two scenarios:

Scenario 1) Jane loves to travel. She has a corporate job that she hates. She feels unappreciated, overworked and underpaid. She works Monday thru Friday and every day is the same. She wakes up at 6:00AM, goes to the gym, showers, then she's off to work. By

Friday, Jane is hitting the snooze button 3 times and missing her workouts at the gym. She knows they are important; however, she is dreading her day. It's the end of her week, she dislikes her job and just wants to stay home.

Scenario 2) Jane loves to travel. Jane was just offered the opportunity to go on a month long safari for an assignment at her job. The downside is she will not get to sleep much as the assignment will require long hours, double the work load and no extra pay. Jane accepts with extreme excitement. She has always wanted to go on a safari. Jane has just worked all day, but has to pack and catch a red eye. She is so excited as she packs and makes her way to the airport. She made it and is settled in for a 10-hour flight. She will have to begin her work as soon as she arrives and will not get much sleep for the next week. Jane is aware of her limitations and the work load, however she can't sleep. She is too excited!

I trust that it's obvious where the resistance is. When we are doing what we love, nothing matters. We can conquer the world. So if you are feeling resistance, explore why. Explore what the root of your resistance is. Go back to the same questions you asked yourself earlier at your mesa. Do the exercise as many times as needed to get to the bottom of what you are resisting and why. When you know what and why, you can explore how to change resistance into an amazing opportunity for change.

One last perspective is how we view our anger. I learned the ABC's of anger from a respected and loved mentor named Gordon Cook. I worked with Gordon when doing a 13 week shamanic, herbalism apprenticeship with Susun Weed. Gordon taught me to recognize the different types of anger:

• A – Anger: Immediate anger, then action. It happened NOW, it's expressed NOW and then it's gone.

o Example: A child throwing a fit. They scream, cry, release and it's over.

• B – Behind the back or bottled up anger: Anger you feel and do not express out of FEAR or powerlessness. Now it compounds as you carry the anger and it starts to come out in different ways.

o Example: A coworker is not pulling their weight, yet he/she is the bosses drinking buddy and you are not.

o Example: A parent/authority figure reprimands you and will not let you explain your position.

• C – Childhood Anger: Trying to fix your childhood by re-creating trauma, hoping for a different outcome. YOU CANNOT CHANGE THE PAST. ACCEPT IT AND MOVE ON.

o Example: You keep dating someone that reminds you of your dad who abandoned you. The men are incapable of loving you the way you need to be loved and they abandon you too. You recreate a relationship with the same person with a different face. You continue to get the same result.

• D- Deflective Anger: Being angry at one person/place/event and taking it out on another.

o   Example: A father feels powerless in his position and was yelled at all day at work. He comes home and takes it out on his kids who are powerless to him.

•   E- Erratic or Exoteric Anger: Angry at the world; No real cause, just angry; very destructive; bad attitude; out of control

o   Example: An alcoholic that is stuck in the disease. Yelling at anyone and everyone for no reason other than in self-destruct mode. Could be exerted verbally or physically. Hitting random things, breaking and throwing things.

Understanding where your anger is coming from will help you move through it. Sometimes we just get angry. Putting together a pattern for your anger will help you break your destructive patterns. Knowing where the anger comes from allows you to choose the right tool to use.

10 NEW TOOLS

Change is a process, not an event.

-    Anonymous

I had been working with Jan and Seth for about a month when I got the call! The magic call in which I was met with excitement rather than panic. Seth said "I did it! And it worked!" I asked "what did you do?" and he was so proud that instead of meeting Jan's anxiety with more anxiety, he paused, took a deep breath, connected to source and centered himself. He then was able to hear Jan's problem. That is really important, he was able to listen and HEAR Jan's problem. He then calmly was able to talk through it with her until finding a solution.

I was so proud and excited!

Seth loved Jan, and in the past when she was upset, he would get upset. He took on her anxiety, pain, or whatever emotions she was feeling. He was trying to help her, only his insecurities turned the situation into something about him, preventing him from recognizing her needs. He felt that he had to fix her problem and would go into panic mode. He didn't really know how to fix it and that would trigger his insecurities and he would create a bigger dilemma for Jan by making it all about what he is trying to do for her. It would usually end up in a fight and more pain for Jan.

Now looking at the before and after, what amazing progress! SO exciting!

The tool Seth chose to use here was his breath and grounding. When we feel flustered, our natural reaction is to talk, fix, act. However, if we react without thinking, we are potentially doing so much more damage. By pausing, taking five very deep breaths, centering and grounding, Seth was able to be present for Jan. Seth was able to clear and calm his mind and think with clarity, allowing him to be present for Jan. Our breath is our most powerful tool. It is always available.

Here are the steps that Seth went through:

- Pause
- Five deep belly breaths
- Drop into heart center
- Clarity that his response is coming from a place of love, not fear
- Calmly speak and act from a heart centered place

It's amazing how different the outcome was from his past reactions. This one tool alone changed the dynamic of their relationship. As they started implementing additional tools we will go over, it got even better.

One of my favorite tools is The Five Love Languages by Gary Chapman. These are brilliant! I first discovered this book when it was recommended to me by a dear friend, Larry. I called Larry, needing help in my relationship at the time and this book cleared up the disconnect as well as helping me communicate more effectively in all my other relationships.

The five love languages are;

- Words of affirmation
- Acts of service
- Receiving gifts
- Quality time
- Physical touch

Knowing how you "feel and receive" love is an essential part of knowing yourself. Being able to apply this to your relationships with others will help you understand them more. Learning to communicate effectively is learning to understand what is important to those you are communicating with.

This is what triggered my thoughts on exploring the golden rule. I truly believe that we must learn to love and communicate with others by learning what feels good for them.

This leads to another wonderful tool for better communication, the integrity check. Before the words come out of your mouth, ask yourself some very powerful questions. When you can answer these with clarity and feel good about your actions, then it's safe to proceed.

- What is my intention?
- Am I saying/doing this from a loving place?
- Does it need to be said?
- Does it need to be said by me?
- Does it need to be said now?
- How would it feel if it were being said/done to me?

These are very powerful questions. Take the time to answer, and answer honestly, BEFORE you act. When you invest this time prior to acting, it saves you so much work. You avoid shame, blame, guilt and all the other emotions that come with reacting. Hurting someone else never feels good. SO, take the time to PAUSE and check yourself. You will be rewarded with a clear conscience.

Some people just want to fight. They antagonize you. It happened a lot to me when I owned my gym. If you find yourself in this position and you need to react or say something, here are two very powerful phrases;

- "Oh", then repeat back what you heard
- "You may be right", then repeat what you heard

These are amazing ways to acknowledge, deflect and still not engage. An example of how these work:

When I owned the gym, it was a small private facility with some amazing massage therapists. We all specialized in our services and catered to the elderly, and special needs population. We were priced according to our expertise. It never failed that clients would come in and complain about the prices and let me know that it was cheaper down the street. They had 2 goals:

• Complaint – they wanted to express their anger for our cost, and they wanted to be heard.

• Attempt to get me to lower the cost of our specialty services to match the prices of non-specialty services.

I would here, "It's cheaper to get a massage at XYZ."

My response, "You may be right, it may be cheaper to get a massage at XYZ."

Them, "Yes, I may go there."

Me, "Oh, you may go there?"

Them, "They have everything you do."

Me, "You may be right, they may have everything I do."

It was crazy, however I would talk in circles with them as long as they stood in my business and demanded it. I was very confident in my prices, my team, my services and I knew my competition. The client was standing in my business fighting me for a reason, yet they needed what we had to offer. They knew it. I knew it.

When you are confident in your actions, your behaviors, yourself, it's so easy to deflect the attacks. You can actually start to have fun with it!

I asked my best friend for examples of some attacks she has heard. I laughed so hard, I had to share! Here are examples, using three phrases to respond:

• Attack: "You are about as handy as a screen door on a

submarine!"

• Response: "You may be right; I may be as handy as a screen door on a submarine."

• Attack: "Do you know how to use your brain?"

• Response: "Oh, you are wondering if I know how to use my brain?"

• Attack: "Are you having a blonde moment?"

• Response: "You may be right; I may be having a blonde moment."

• Attack: "Is your butt jealous from the amount of crap coming out of your mouth?"

• Response: "Oh, you think my butt is jealous of the crap coming out of my mouth!"

When people are not looking for an argument, they often just want to be heard and acknowledged. It is very simple to respond to this with "I hear you".

I often refer to this behavior as the human trash dump. People need to unload whatever garbage they are experiencing. They are not necessarily looking for a solution; they just want to vent. Their objective is to find someone to acknowledge their pain/anger/frustration and then sympathize with them. It is very easy when you do not take it personally, do not engage, and just say "I hear you". If you have not used this simple phrase before, you will love it. It will change the dynamics of all your relationships. You have no need to fix anyone, and they will appreciate you more for not trying. They will respect and appreciate you for the simple act of listening and hearing them. It truly is a game changer!!!!

I HEAR YOU.

You are holding the space for them to release and LET IT GO. How amazing is that? It is a liberating experience!

All of these tools are freeing your mind. You are creating new thought patterns. You are retraining your brain to breathe vs react. You are retraining yourself not to engage, but to listen, acknowledge, and hear others. You are consciously breaking your cycles and creating healthier experiences. You are now choosing to be part of the solution. It's so beautiful, and I am so proud of you. I know that you are already feeling more at peace. Your life and your relationships are improving. Your ability to communicate is improving. These tools are allowing you to slow down, clarify and make smarter choices.

I said this in the beginning of the book, however, I am going to say it again since it is important. Your thoughts and beliefs become your actions. Your actions become your habits. Your habits become your reality, your character, YOU. You are a co-creator of your reality through your thoughts, beliefs and actions. SO, how can you change your reality? By changing your thoughts and beliefs. Change your self-talk. It is as important to communicate with yourself as clearly as you communicate with others. Do not get bogged down by your own self talk. You are the creator of your reality. We will go over more strategies on this subject in future chapters.

One of the hardest things for me to learn was PAUSE and LISTEN. Be SILENT. I struggled with this one for a long time. I struggled because my EGO was out of control. I learned this through my shadow-self work. My natural reaction was to defend myself. I wanted to prove I was right or they were wrong. The result: I looked guilty and created more chaos in my life.

There is absolutely NO REASON to defend yourself. This is another form of unhealthy communication. If you feel your defenses bubbling up:

STOP. Breath. Connect.

Ask yourself, why I am reacting? There could be several answers. Here are some things to think about:

- Am I being falsely accused?
  - If so, defending yourself in the moment will only make you look guilty. You cannot rationalize with someone that is irrational. You are better off staying silent and allowing them to release whatever they need to release. Your defense will only increase the intensity of the attack. Stay silent or use the deflection techniques we discussed earlier.
  - If not, admit your part of the problem. Take ownership of your actions. Do what needs to be done from a loving place to rectify the problem. If you were wrong, move through it

as calmly and honestly as possible. It may be painful, however you will be able to sleep at night. Taking responsibility for our wrong doings allows us and those we hurt to move past the situation and begin to heal.

- What is this situation reminding me of?
- What can I learn about this person? What is their attack teaching me about where they are in their head right now? You can learn so much about a person by listening to them.
- What am I afraid of right now?
- What is the worst that can happen?
- How can I calm myself and the situation?
- Can I just walk away?
- Does this make sense?
- What questions can I ask to clarify the situation?

Reacting will only create a situation in which both parties are now irrational and not thinking clearly. Pausing, breathing, and staying silent will allow you to find clarity of the situation. Silence will allow you to look at the entire situation objectively from an outside point of view. Staying silent will allow you to observe your feelings, emotions, and move through them with grace. The more you can contain your reactions, observe your emotions, and understand yourself, the easier it will be to communicate with others. You will have clarity or at least have the ability to ask the right questions to find clarity of the situation.

Your silence allows you to move through the chaos without creating more. It allows you to connect to a heart centered place and view the situation objectively. You can then respond from a loving place with grace and dignity. You will be able to effectively communicate using all the tools you have learned. This will eliminate misunderstandings, hurt feelings, regrets, etc. You will be clear and calm. Your messages will be heard and understood. People will appreciate you and respect you as you leave them feeling heard and acknowledged.

Communication can make or break a relationship. Use these tools to make your relationships and interactions healthy, loving, respectful experiences for both you and the people you encounter. As the saying goes:

People will not always remember what you said, but they will remember how you made them feel.

11 RELATIONSHIPS

The road to resentments is paved with expectations.

- Anonymous

To set the tone for this chapter, Halloween is my favorite holiday. I LOVE dressing up! My best friend and I were going to a party, so I invited an ex-boyfriend of mine, Billy, to join us. Billy and I had not been dating for quite some time, however we were talking again, rebuilding a friendship. Billy wanted more, I was open to seeing how much he had changed during our time apart.

Billy needed a costume and had asked for my assistance shopping. I agreed. I had a costume that I could wear, not much money, and was willing to make what I had work. We went for the sole purpose of finding Billy a costume.

The store we went to was an old supermarket building, it was huge! I was so excited to explore. I had no intentions of buying anything, however, I loved to look! Billy asked for my opinion and I expressed that I wanted to explore the entire store and all the possibilities before giving him my opinion. He acknowledged my request and we set out on our paths to discovering the costume possibilities!

Several times throughout the shopping experience Billy approached me with different ideas he had and to see where my thoughts were. I gave him a thumbs up on what he showed me and continued to explore. For me, it was just an exciting experience to get more and more ideas and see the fun costumes. We both knew my funds were low and I was going to make do with what I had. I was there for support, enjoying the journey.

Billy had found his costume. He pulled me over to get my opinion and assist him with accessories. I was enjoying showing him all the possibilities I thought would go great with his choice. He was Robin Hood and we were exploring bows, arrows, head pieces and tights! We picked a winning outfit and Billy was going to try it on.

Right before Billy went to the dressing room, he cornered me. He knew how much I loved costumes. He made sure to have my full attention and said, "I know you don't have much money and are struggling right now. I want this to be fun tomorrow night. I want this to be a great experience for you. I will buy you a costume. I want you to feel that I've changed. I am showing you I have changed. I am showing you......"

He was showing me he had not changed at all. I share this because it's important to see that he was doing what served him and made him feel special. Cornering me and pointing out my financial struggle, on no level, was making me feel loved, special, or creating an enjoyable experience for me. He wanted so desperately to be my hero. Buying me a costume was for him, so he could feel like he saved the day, not for me.

One of the most powerful quotes I ever heard is this:

Why am I so empty that I am so full of you?
-Anonymous

Really think about that quote for a minute. Let it sink in and resonate with you.

What does it bring up? How does it make you feel? Does it make you question who you invest the majority of your time thinking about? Does it make you question why that time, energy, love, is not invested in YOU.

Relationships are tough. Every relationship, not just love. However, when we are in an intimate relationship, and we are empty inside, it's deadly. If you are not 100% full of self-love, self-worth, and the ability to be true to yourself, YOU SHOULD NOT BE IN A RELATIONSHIP. You cannot have a healthy, loving relationship with another human being until you have a healthy, loving relationship with yourself.

Take the story I just shared with you. Billy needs to be needed, and seeks approval. He so desperately was puking his needs on me by seeking my adoration. He couldn't let me enjoy wandering the store and doing what made me happy, because he wanted attention. HE needed me to know he was willing to buy me something. HE needed me to acknowledge him. HE needed me to know that he was willing to buy me something. HE needed to hear me say thank you. NONE of that behavior was for me at all. It did not help me feel special, it felt horrible. I had a costume I would have been fine wearing. I LOVE Halloween and was enjoying walking the isles and looking at all the fun stuff. I was truly enjoying myself. HIS constant need to see if I found something so he could be my hero and buy it was distracting and exhausting. That constant NEED is exactly why he is my EX. It was a constant in our relationship.

In the beginning, I also had very unhealthy NEEDS. I was attracted to him because he had money and power. I thought I was somehow incapable of achieving that on my own. My faulty programming and belief system had convinced me that I was not enough. I believed I NEEDED a man. I believed I NEEDED a man to take care of me. I believed I NEEDED, rather than believing I AM ENOUGH.

This constant battle and NEED caused only destruction and pain. We both were convinced we LOVED each other. However, now I believe that you cannot truly love another until you COMPLETELY love yourself. Until you are 100% full of self-love, you cannot fully love another. Believing we can love another before fully loving ourselves is a lie we tell ourselves. It's a lie that allows us to stay stuck. It's a lie that helps us fill our void by loving another the way we want to be loved. Instead of looking in the mirror and seeing the pain, emptiness and void in our self, we unconsciously attract someone with our holes. We then try to fill the holes in that person and pat ourselves on the back for all we have done. It's toxic, self-defeating behavior.

Billy and I have had a toxic relationship for about 3 years. We attempted to heal together. I chose to get sober while living with him. It was IMPOSSBLE. We both had so much self-work to do, it was NOT possible to do the work and stay together. We both loved the other and cared about each other. However, I have already expressed that this is not possible. I loved Billy, until MY need became more important, at which point, I hurt Billy. Billy loved me, until HIS need became more important, and then he verbally attacked and attempted to destroy me. When I was upset and hurt, I walked away in an attempt to cool down and clear my head. Billy had abandonment issues. Therefore, when I left the house to cool down, he would follow. If I got in the car and drove away, he got in a car and followed. If he hurt, he made sure I hurt. He was convinced that I would never return. His inability to trust me or give me my space ultimately destroyed us.

I quickly learned that all that money and power I was attracted to was the biggest illusion I had ever been lost in. What I soon learned was that it was a destructive illusion of a very damaged man. He was not confident, rich and powerful. He was a terrified, damaged boy that had learned how to create an illusion and make people need him. He learned how to make people need him, even if they didn't like him, in order to prevent anyone from abandoning him ever again.

This ultimately destroyed him. It destroyed us. It was destroying his relationship with his son. He was so deep in his illusion that he even treated his 6-year-old son this way. His son was terrified of him. His son was being programmed to do what dad expects and make dad happy, or be punished. His son was becoming a robot.

I share all of this because we truly have no idea how much we damage others by our own false thinking. If we really take a deep and honest look at what we are doing and why, then examine the results, they usually do not line up at all. The majority of the time, the results we are getting are the opposite. This happens because we operate from a fear based place rather than a love based place. When we truly love another human being, we only want them to feel loved, safe, joy, and bliss. However, we cannot emanate something we do not have. If I don't love myself, how can I show love to another?

Here's another great example: I have gone through some horrible times in which I was financially broke. I have had other times when I was making plenty of money. I love helping people. It was a friend's birthday; he didn't have any family around, he was struggling financially and was really just down and out. I was not in a great place financially, however, I had a little extra and wanted to make his day special. I picked him up and took him out to eat. At the restaurant he was looking at prices and feeling insecure about getting what he wanted. I expressed, I am paying, get whatever you want. It's your birthday, treat yourself. He did and the smile on his face was priceless. We then proceeded to go shopping at Party City. Remember, I love Halloween, so I create reasons to dress up! So we went in, tried on costumes, crazy hats, had a blast. I ended up buying him a costume, myself a costume and one for my best friend who was not able to be with us. We dressed up that night and had a blast.

My self-love, self-worth, and resources were completely full and I was able to give. This friend had NO expectations and was happy with a phone call from me. He NEEDED nothing and was filled with gratitude. Giving to him was my choice. It was not expected and it was completely appreciated. It actually filled my self-love to be able to give. It was a gift and we never discussed it again.

Another scenario is with Billy. He eats more than most people. When I let him back into my life, he spent time with me and my roommate. I love to cook healthy food. I didn't have much money, but I did spend extra to buy healthy and organic. I like to cook in bulk so I have left overs. I would create magical meals for all of us, using the last of all the food I had. I did this often for my roommate and me and the food would last a week. When Billy came, I cooked twice as much, and we had almost nothing left. He ate everything. Every time he came over, he ate. I continued to share, and he continued to take.

I had to start setting boundaries and expressing that he needed to participate by sharing and bringing supplies. It is not my responsibility to feed him, nor could I afford to feed him. He understood, and brought food. He then took all the extra with him when he left!!!

Are you starting to see the pattern? I was starting to get very resentful and angry. This was entirely MY fault for not setting the boundaries. I knew how much he ate. I knew he had no idea how much love, energy, money, and self I put into shopping, prepping, cooking, etc. I had experienced him showing up, inhaling, and looking for more. It was a pattern. This pattern was not just with food; it was our entire relationship. I felt completely unappreciated. I take full responsibility. I needed to set boundaries.

As I began setting boundaries, I was faced with much resistance. I quickly learned how much the new boundaries would be challenged. It was a painful process. When you allow others to take and take until they drain you completely, they do not like being cut off. However, if they actually do care for you, they will eventually respect the new boundaries. If they don't, **BE GRATEFUL!**

Be grateful that you loved yourself enough to stop allowing someone else to highjack your energy. Be grateful that your new boundaries are teaching you to protect yourself. Be grateful your new boundaries are showing you who your true friends really are. Be grateful your new boundaries are eliminating the leaches from your life. Be grateful you are loving yourself enough.

Learning to set boundaries is HARD. It is a very scary process. It creates so much fear. Fear of loss, fear of no longer being accepted, fear of not being loved, fear of so much. We are terrified that someone may no longer like us, or be mad at us. Think about that for a minute.

We are scared that if we protect ourselves, love ourselves and stop giving what we do not have, that we will be rejected. How messed up is that? How insane is it that we allow another human being to deplete and disrespect us, and then fear the loss of them if we decide to love ourselves enough?

This is what happens in relationships until we are full of ourselves.

Sometimes this process earns us the label selfish. You are selfish because you are taking your time for your healing, your needs, and protecting yourself. That is not selfish, that is self-worth. When you are in an airplane, they say "put your mask on first. You must save yourself before you can save another" If you have a child and pass out while putting the mask on them, because you didn't put yours on first...how the heck are you going to save your child? Life is the same challenging way. How on earth can you love, help, and give to another when you are an empty broken soul? **YOU CAN'T**.

So healthy boundaries are a necessity. We teach others how to treat us by what we accept and what we allow. Please understand that statement, it's the most important line in this book.

WE TEACH OTHERS HOW TO TREAT US BY WHAT WE ACCEPT AND WHAT WE ALLOW.

When you do not set a boundary and you do not tell someone their behavior is unacceptable, they do not know. They will continue to treat you that way until you STOP accepting it. This can all be expressed in a loving way. For example, when I am cooking, I cook without expectations of leftovers, and with the understanding that I am giving it all away or I don't cook. I also tell others what I will be providing and what my expectations are from them if they plan to attend. I tell people exactly what I want and need them to bring. They then have the choice to participate under the parameters of my boundaries and by honoring my request, or they can choose not to attend. I do not feel guilty if someone chooses not to attend. I am filled with gratitude for those who respect my boundaries, honor my investment, bring something to the table and co-create an amazing evening with me. It is a much different experience than I used to feel. There is no more resentment or anger. I no longer feel taken advantage of. I created the boundaries and experience I wanted. I loved myself enough to say, this is what I NEED for this to be harmonious for all involved. I was very clear on my expectations and I stood my ground with love. Love for both myself and all involved.

This chapter has been more story filled than the rest. I felt it was the best way to deliver the message. Talking about boundaries is very boring. So let me breakdown and sum up the overall message. The first relationship you need is with yourself. When you have a healthy relationship with yourself, meaning a healthy understanding of your needs, then the rest will fall into place.

Pay attention to your needs. If you are being challenged, ask yourself, is this my need or someone else's need? If you are being triggered by someone or feel the need to help them in a certain way, look in the mirror. We are triggered by things we need to heal in our self. What you are being drawn to most likely is a reflection of what you are choosing to not face in yourself. Why are you choosing to not acknowledge that part of you?

Listen to what people are saying. On the same level that your desires and actions are a self-reflection, so are theirs. Listen instead of reacting. Don't make what they are saying and doing about you. Instead, try to really listen. You will learn what they are going through. Our natural tendency is to make it about ourselves, react and defend. STOP. LISTEN. They are telling you exactly where they are and what they are fighting. It has NOTHING to do with you.

When you are feeling unappreciated or taken advantage of, STOP. GO within, look at what you are feeling. Clarify what you need from the situation. Clarify what you are experiencing. What do you need to happen differently in order to feel appreciated, loved, respected, and for this to be a healthy experience? Once you figure that out, communicate it. In the most loving way possible, express how the situation made you feel, communicate what is acceptable and how you need this to happen in the future. Lovingly communicate what behavior will no longer be acceptable to you. Communicate this in a way that is not blaming or accusing the other person. Keep it to your needs. Then stand your ground, honor yourself, and those who care will honor your needs. Let go of those who do not. It's ok, you are better off without them. You are setting the boundaries that you will only accept healthy experiences that honor both you and the people in your life.

When you are full of self-love, self-worth, and have healthy boundaries, your life will change. Your relationships will change. ALL of your relationships. They all start with you. As you grow and mold yourself, the people you attract will follow your lead. The more you love, honor and respect yourself.... the more the people around you will love, honor and respect you.

12 PLAN AHEAD

"Obstacles are those frightful things you see when you take your
eyes off the goal."

- Henry Ford

You have done so much work, let's set you up for success. You
are going to encounter roadblocks, setbacks, obstacles. What are you
going to do? You are going to have a plan in place to move through,
around, past.

I AM. The most powerful words we can say. These are the words
that plant the seeds to our future. What we think becomes what we
believe. What we believe determines how we feel. How we feel
directly effects how we function. So what does all this mean to me,
you ask? Thank you for asking, I would love to make it simple. Our
thoughts become our beliefs. Our beliefs determine our feelings. Our
feelings direct our actions. Our actions become our reality. So, our
thoughts become reality. Now ask yourself, what am I thinking?

What reality am I creating for myself?

Planting the seeds of success, abundance, and self-love are the most empowering thoughts we can plant for ourselves. However, it is not just about planting these beautiful thoughts in our mind, we have to nourish these ideas we plant. A perfect example would be a beautiful garden we would like to grow. If we just put the seeds in the ground and forget them, will they grow? Depends, if mother nature provides the perfect amount of rain and sun creating the perfect environment for each seed, that would be ideal. However, there are periods of extended rain, followed be extreme drought. There are days of endless sun followed by a hurricane. Depending on an outside source for our desired results does not sound like the best option. Are you willing to bet the odds on perfect conditions, and risk all your beautiful energy, love, and commitment not flourishing? Or would you prefer to take the proactive approach and nourish your seeds daily? Personally, I would rather invest a small amount of time daily to ensure that all of my seeds grow into the beautiful garden that I planned. I cannot think, wish or meditate this growth, I must take the necessary action for my garden to reach its fullest potential.

Our mind is the same as our garden. It does not matter how many thoughts, meditations, vision boards, or affirmations we create. These are all step one, the seeds, the clarity of where we need to focus our energy. This clarity must be followed by actions that nurture these goals toward flourishing into the experiences we desire. Experiences can only happen when we create the environment that invites and welcomes the desired experience. Examine a garden. If I wish to grow a garden providing all of my own food, that would be an amazing gift. However, if this is a seed in my meditation, without action, how would it happen? I have to actually buy the seeds, plant them in the dirt, hold the space with love, and nourish the growth. This takes time, effort, love, and patience.

So how does this garden relate to me and I AM. Creating a vision of what you truly desire will determine a clear path. Meditating on the details, feeling the outcome, knowing that anything is possible connects you with source. It puts you in the mindset of unlimited potential. Now you have the clarity, direction and the mindset. You are in the perfect position to take action. As you flow through life, you can ask yourself, is this taking me toward my desired experience or away from my desired experience? You will have the clarity to move through your day with ease. Knowing what outcome, you desire opens up unlimited help from the universe. As you keep your energy and actions aligned with your goals, you will notice that things just start to fall into place. It starts to feel so easy, effortless and blissful. All you want keeps merging into your reality with less and less effort. You are aligning energetically with the experiences you most desire, effortlessly.

This does not mean there will not be roadblocks in the path. There might be a flood or a hurricane. What then? This is where your tools, a positive attitude, and an ability to be flexible are invaluable. When you operate from a place of clarity, these setbacks no longer become overwhelming and destructive obstacles. Instead, they are the most amazing opportunities. Opportunities to grow and experience strength and wisdom you may not have realized you possess. You are an empowered, strong and magical human being that is completely capable of weathering even what seems like the most impossible storm. You have the power inside you. You have all the answers within. All you have to do is tap into that place, that inner vault. The place where you planted the seeds and you have been loving and nourishing up until this point. You are prepared to handle anything with grace, dignity, and ease.

Many times when we meet these challenges, we ask why me? Why is this happening to me? Why am I so broke? Why is my life out of control?

Here's the key, THE UNIVERSE WILL ANSWER THE QUESTIONS YOU ASK! Yup, that's the key! So what do you need to do? Ask better questions. Yes, it's that simple. Ask for what you want instead of answers as to why not!

Here are some fabulous questions to ask:

• Why am I so abundant?

• Why do I meet the most amazing people?

• How do I keep getting so fortunate?

• Why is my life so blessed?

• How lucky am I that my life is filled with love?

Ask the questions you want answered and then listen. Let the universe guide you. Keep all this in mind as you now map out your vision. You are going to manifest the life you desire by creating your vision.

Creating your vision is going to start with a vision board. Your vision board is going to have the right questions and affirmations to awaken that seed inside you. You can create a vision board with pictures of what you think you want now…. Or you can allow me to challenge you to create a vision bigger, better and more amazing than you can comprehend at this time! I know it sounds weird, but humor me for long enough to understand my request.

I have made three vision boards and I achieved/acquired and got everything I thought I wanted. The problem was my vision was limited to my understanding at that time. So we are going to create your vision board using your new questions to the universe. You are going to create a limitless vision. How exciting is that?

If you want a fancy car or have specific desires, please add them. Keep you vision true to you. This exercise is for YOUR future and you are creating your dream life. So always be true to you. The part I am going to challenge you to add is this:

If you are unsure in certain areas, then have gratitude for what you desire.

- I am grateful for more abundance than I can comprehend at this time.
- I am grateful for more love and laughter than I knew existed.
- I am grateful for the opportunity to serve more people in ways that I did not understand possible.
- Thank you for showing me what I do not even know to ask for.
- Thank you for guiding me to people, places and things that I would not have thought of.

- Thank you for blessing me with a life that is more amazing than I could have dreamt of.

I think you are getting the idea. If you have specifics, absolutely set your vision on what you know in your heart you want. All I ask is that you not limit yourself to your understanding at this time.

Another fun thing to keep you on track is notes to yourself. I write notes and set alarms to remind myself all the time. Here are some fun things to set you up for success:

- Mirror talk: Take dry erase markers and write on your mirrors or windows.
    - I AM Love
    - I AM light
    - I AM abundant
    - Gratitude is my Attitude
- Write notes and tape them to your fridge or on your TV
    - Did you work out today?
    - Break through, don't break down
    - You are strong, remember what you're working for
    - You are beautiful, love yourself enough, it starts within
- Set reminders on your phone, especially if you are having a challenging day.
    - You are beautiful
    - Have I told you I LOVE YOU today
    - Love is all that exists

- Don't be afraid to ask for help
  - I gave my friends permission to call me out on my BS
  - Set up a support group and have people to call if you get in a funk
- Go to meetings

- Put a dry erase board or chalk board up

- List things you need to do

- Free your mind by writing it down

- Prioritize

- Write yourself more love notes

You should be well on your way to successfully navigating roadblocks and obstacles at this point. You have put so much love and energy into your success! I am so proud of you for taking the time to invest in yourself. You are so worth it and your future will reflect all of your hard work.

13 CHOOSING A COACH OR MENTOR

CLARITY

Credible Leadership, Authentic Reliable Integrity,
Trust Yourself

\-   Willow Green

There are two women in my life that I have tremendous gratitude for. I hired both at separate times in my life. Neither woman was on my radar when I found them, I was guided to them by spirit and my inner compass. When I found them I asked spirit, "Am I meant to work with this woman?". I asked spirit very specific questions and for very specific signs that I was meant to hire each woman. I had little money and little coming in at the time. Hiring them would require a huge leap of faith on my part. Faith that the money would show up and it would all work out. Though I have tremendous gratitude for what I learned, I had two very different experiences.

The first woman is Susun Weed. I was lead to Susun through a psychic telling me I was going to be an herbalist. I laughed, I had no idea what an herbalist was at the time. However, I have a deep faith and trust that spirit will guide me if I listen and follow the signs. So, I went home and started researching herbalism.

I came across several programs. Then I came across Susun Weed. She had many options to work with her. I chose to apply for her Shamanic Herbal Apprenticeship for the longest option of 13 weeks. This program required that I live with Susun in New York for the entire 13 weeks. I would surrender my thoughts, ideas, attitudes, beliefs, etc. I had to show up with an open mind and willingness to do what Susun taught for the entire program.

Susun interviews you. You have to apply, interview, and be accepted to work with her. During the interview process, she tries to talk you out of coming. You have to want to change. You have to be ready to change. She warns that living with her will not be easy. She warns, "you will cry, you will want to run." She is transparent, raw and honest. She wants you there if, and only if, you want to be there and you are ready to be deprogrammed and empowered. To work with Susun, you have to have trust and strength. She warns that she will test you, push you, pull you and you will feel lost, confused, challenged and it will not be easy or fun.

She was right. Living with Susun was one of the hardest things that I have ever done. It was also one of the greatest gifts I could have ever given myself. Susun warns you of the challenge, yes. What Susun does not tell you is how much love she has. She has dedicated her life to educating and empowering women. She is the strongest, most amazing woman I have ever met. She embodies so much wisdom and love, more than I knew existed. There is nothing that she does that does not come from her heart. At times I felt fear, confusion, anger, and many other emotions when living with her. I did want to run at times. Many women who choose to work with her do run. She will tell you, "if you don't want to run, she's not doing her job. If you do run, you are not doing your job." She's right. I stayed. I did my job.

I know now, Susun was very aware of EVERYTHING that went on at her house. She always had my back along with every woman that has ever invested in themselves by trusting her. Every move Susun made was to make me stronger, wiser and to teach me. She was so conscious of making sure I was safe, nourished, loved and cared for. Yes, the lessons were challenging, however they came with love. I have never, before living with Susun or after, felt as safe, loved, nourished, and protected as I did during those 13 weeks.

What I gained was priceless. I gained wisdom, self-worth, self-love, self-awareness and learned so much about myself. I learned about my shadow self. I learned to nourish myself. I learned to love and honor myself. I learned how to use my voice with honor and grace. It was the most amazing 13 weeks of my life. I learned to trust myself.

I have so much love, respect and gratitude for Susun. She is an inspiration. I honor her for her love of empowering women. Susun holds space and allows women to blossom. She challenges them to empower them. Susun truly operates from her heart and is one of my favorite people.

The second woman is Angela Lauria. I found Angela the same way I found Susun and was instantly drawn to her. I couldn't get an interview for over a month, and that was not going to work for me! So I sent her an email explaining that I was ready now and did not have a month to waste. I asked spirit to make it happen if I was meant to work with Angela. The next day we were on the phone and I hired her! There was no question it was meant to be!

I hired Angela to help me write this book. During our interview we discussed when my manuscript would be finished and the next book launch date. My understanding at the time was that I was going to write this book and be published in 3 months! I understood that the launch date would be MY launch date. I was so excited!

The process was intense. I was very lost at the start and worked through so many crazy thoughts and ideas. I challenged Angela. I was very skeptical and questioned so much of the process. I felt like I was trying so hard and just couldn't figure it out. It was frustrating. The others in the program encouraged me to trust Angela and trust the process. I did and I pushed through with everything I had. I shut up. I showed up and I did the work.

Once I surrendered and found my flow, miracles started happening. It was amazing. It was like my book was writing itself! I got completely lost in what I was creating and making sure it was going to be of service. My only goal is to empower others and that is the goal of this book.

The day I finished my book was the best and worst day of this experience. I finished and asked what next? I wanted to get started with the editing. I was making plans for the holidays, and reached out to confirm my book launch date of December 15. I did not receive the confirmation and became increasingly confused. I couldn't figure out why Angela was not telling me what was going on.

She referred me to a video for more information. The video talked about the publishing options. What I learned was that to actually publish with her it was going to cost me another 3x my investment. I felt like I was going to puke. I filled up with anger, fear, and disgust. I felt lied to and betrayed. The thought of Angela made me sick. I couldn't believe she intentionally mislead me. I had raved about this woman and felt deliberately mislead. I wanted nothing more to do with her.

We have group meetings online and ironically this all happened about an hour before the meeting. I was having a breakdown. I tried to hide it, but I couldn't. I cried to the group about all kinds of stuff. I was feeling very vulnerable, duped, and scared. I made my drama about everything other than the truth. I was scared to express my truth to Angela and tell her just how pissed I was that she sold me a false picture. I was angry, and for some reason unable to verbalize what I was actually going through. She talked me through my emotions. I can honestly say that was my last melt down. What she taught me in that moment was that I no longer need meltdowns. Life is full of ups, downs, challenges and obstacles. I know this. I also know I will learn and it will pass, there's absolutely no reason for my meltdowns. They no longer serve me and they are gone. I am so grateful for that lesson.

Over the next couple weeks, I thought long and hard about how to deal with the situation. The story I told makes me a victim and Angela a seller of illusions. I thought about that a lot. I used my own tools. I looked at the situation from a new perspective. I asked myself, is that story real? My answer was no. Angela didn't lie at all, she shared truths, they just weren't my truths. There were signs and red flags that I chose not to see. She was giving me information and I was taking what I wanted to hear. Looking back, it's all so clear to me now. I needed to be misled. Had I not believed that everything was included, I would have seen the price tag and never signed up. I would have been paralyzed by my financial fear and this book never would have been written. I would not have developed my full potential.

I choose to love Angela. Without her, I would not have found my voice. She did exactly what she promised me she would do. She held the space. She holds space for success and breakthroughs. Failure is not an option. I am grateful to have had the opportunity to learn from her. She pushed me to a new all-time high and for that, I am extremely grateful.

I learned so much about myself in this process as well. Angela lives in a castle and has beautiful parties. She creates this amazing red carpet event for the authors who publish with her. It's the complete star treatment with professional hairstylists and make-up artists to glam everyone up. She then interviews everyone on camera about their book and really promotes them with so much love and excitement. This is part of what drew me in. Interestingly, it no longer calls me or attracts me. I learned that I really prefer to be barefoot, braless and in a field or forest somewhere! I feel much more at home in nature, no glam. Again, I am so grateful for the learning experience.

Angela has a gift. She can truly teach you how to find your inner author, nourish it and allow your voice to come to life. She also has a gift for helping you transform into the best version of yourself. I am so grateful for all that I have learned from her.

Both of these women were the best gifts I could have given myself. I was not investing in them, I invested in me. I chose to hire them. I chose to show up and I chose to do the work. Every mentor we choose, we choose for a very distinct reason. We may not understand the reason at first, however if we continue to show up, it will present itself. The best coaches will be the ones you really dislike at times! They will challenge you and push you to force you out of your comfort zone. They tell you the truth, not what you want to hear. The truth hurts. Acknowledging it and moving through opens you up to your fullest potential. The moment you want to run, that is when the real work begins. If you choose to run, you will miss out. If you choose to work, that is when the real growth happens. You get out of it what you put into it.

I have only love and gratitude for both Susun and Angela. They were priceless teachers. Many times I was so angry at both. I took deep breaths until my anger faded and I could see clearly. When my mind was clear, thankful is all I was left with. They were not the problem, I was!!!! When I took ownership of my limited perspective and broadened my view, I saw what they were teaching me. The biggest challenge is to get out of your own way. Get out of your way and do not get stuck in the anger. Learn to move quickly to a state of gratitude for the lesson. You are doing it for you, your anger doesn't hurt them, it only hurts you.

I have made a lot of mistakes. I have learned a lot of lessons. I have gratitude for each and every one. Even if the lesson hurts, it's valuable. It is how we grow. It is how we learn. The hardest lessons to learn are the lessons that make us stronger. How we handle the lesson is what builds our character. I am choosing gratitude for both women. Both taught me so much.

14 CONCLUSION

END

Explore New Direction

-Willow Green

Congratulations! You have really taken the time to look deep into yourself. It is a huge investment in your future. All of the work you have done is not easy. Having done the challenging work myself, I know what it takes. It takes courage, strength, willingness, and dedication. The amazing thing is…. YOU have all of those incredible qualities, and so many more. I am so proud of you and all the effort you have put into really knowing yourself.

Please take the time to reflect on your experience while reading this book. It's really important that you grasp everything you have gained. The gift of self-awareness is one of the greatest gifts you can give yourself. You should have a very clear understanding of who you are at this time. Please don't mistake clarity of "who you are" with an unrealistic expectation of having all the answers and life all figured out. The goal isn't to have all the answers, but to know how to move forward in a more productive and graceful manner.

The new tools you have implemented into your daily grind are showing you that by changing your behavior, you change your experiences. The less you "react" to what life throws your way, the less chaos you encounter. The more you choose to slow down and breath, the more peaceful your life has become. You are learning how much power you have to control your experiences.

Please do NOT confuse

power to control your reactions

With

power to control outside events, circumstances, or other people.

We do NOT have control over outside forces, other people, and what happens to us. We do however have the power to control how we REACT to people, situations, and adversity. We have the power to decide how we are going to experience each event. We have the power by choosing our reaction, our attitude, and to have gratitude. Gratitude and anger cannot exist in the same mind.

Every minute you have a choice. You can choose to engage or you can choose to breath. You can choose to allow the fear to take over or you can choose to trust and act from a place of love. You can choose to have tunnel vision or you can choose to see another perspective. You can choose to have an open heart and an open mind. You can choose to react or to use any of the new tools you have learned. You can choose to love yourself enough. You can choose to nourish yourself. You can choose. You always have a choice.

Here's a little exercise that may help you when you get stuck. Go out and fill a bucket with rocks. Wash the rocks so you can write on them. Get a sharpie and pull the rocks out one by one. On each rock, write down whatever keeps you stuck. Your list of resentments.

For example:

- Fear
- Unhealthy Boundaries
- Anger
- Envy

Take each of those rocks you have written something on and put them in a bag. Carry it around with you. It's heavy, huh? Yes, all that stuff you carry around is heavy and there is NO need. Take your bag to the ocean (or a lake, the woods, a field, whatever is near you). Set the bag down. Pull the rocks out, one by one. With each rock, read what you wrote. Feel what you wrote. Tell yourself, you are ready to release it. Throw the rock into the ocean and let it go. Feel the release. Let it all go. Do this with each rock until you have let everything go. You have released yourself of everything. Your bag is empty. You are FREE.

Now, imaging yourself walking along the beach enjoying a beautiful day. You look down and see one of your rocks. YOU HAVE A CHOICE. You can choose to pick it back up or you can choose to have gratitude and walk on by.

This is your new way of life. You get to choose what you pick up and allow back into your life. You have worked so hard to release all the excess emotions, fears, baggage, and things that no longer serve you. You have learned to take care of yourself, nourish yourself, love yourself first. You have the tools to move through situations differently. You have your breath. You always have your breath. You have the ability to see life through a new perspective. You have a plan. You have a goal. You have your mesa. You are asking the right questions. You are on your way to the life of your dreams. You have prepared yourself for roadblocks and obstacles. You are unstoppable. You are strong. You can accomplish anything. You have everything you need inside you. You can tap into your inner guidance anytime.

I offer mentorship programs for those seeking more guidance and support. For more information, I invite you to schedule a complimentary discovery call speak with me directly. Please email me to set up your appointment at GroovyWillowGreen@gmail.com.

TESTIMONIALS

"Before working with Willow I had a good life. I come from a family that loves me. I had a fantastic education through the college level. I had traveled all over the world, seen amazing things, and met wonderful people. I had been in relationships, some of them loving, for a time. But none of that mattered, because it seemed no matter how many people I dated, no matter how many beautiful places I explored, or how much I threw myself into learning- I always ended up in the same cycle of self-loathing and destruction. I couldn't see the foundation of love in my life because I didn't know how to love myself. I didn't have the tools I needed to break the cycle of ancestral wounding, learned behavior, and addiction. So I would just ride the cycle out, getting to the peak and thinking maybe this time I won't plummet down again. And then falling down deeper than I ever had before. It was terrifying, and lonely, and a part of me thought I would never find a way past it. That maybe that was just how life was.

I heard an interview with Willow on Susun Weed's herbal health advice podcast. It was during one of darkest periods of my life. I had just completed a difficult and messy relationship ending in a miscarriage, was drinking heavily with the excuse of numbing the pain, and living back home with my family because the people who raised me were both diagnosed with cancer within 3 months of each other. I was a mess. And I knew if I was going to survive my own head, let alone the very normal ebbs and flows of life, something had to change. So I called her for a free 30 minute consultation and it was one of the best decisions I have ever made for myself.

My experience working with Willow reverberated through every aspect of my life. She has simple, effective tools learned through hard won experience and everything she does is imbued with an incredible amount of love. In fact, in certain ways, she redefined the whole concept of love for me. Before, there were pieces of me that felt if I took time to myself, and stood firm in my boundaries and self-care that I was being selfish, not self-loving. So I spent a good majority of my time feeling resentful because I wasn't honoring my own needs. Working with Willow shifted my entire inner landscape so I had the capacity to "meet life on life's terms" as Willow would say. And this has been true, the outer landscape of my life has not actually changed that much. What has changed, thanks to Willow Green, is my perspective of myself. A fundamental shift that, in truth, changes everything.

I would highly recommend working with Willow for anyone who feels lost within the labyrinth that our lives can sometimes appear to be. She is not the guide, because each life is different, but she can show you how to access your own inner map. So you can begin rising to the challenges of life, instead of being bulldozed by them."

- Gabrielle S.

"Willow is dedicated to supporting others on their journey to wholeness and remembering their own power. Witnessing Willow coaching others, encouraged me to hire her as a life coach. I decided to hire her because my own life needed some empowerment. I felt empowered in my career but when it came to my relationships, my sense of personal power disappeared. When I saw her speaking confidently to empower herself and others, I was inspired.

Willow went beyond my expectations as a life coach. She held me accountable to my goals, talked me through tough situations, allowed me to see how I could speak confidently with compassion for myself and others. Because of the coaching I did with Willow, I stepped into bigger leadership roles in my career and manifested experiences better than I had dreamed. In my relationships, I found better ways of communicating and asking for what I need from others. This allowed me to have more fulfilling relationships and the ones that weren't, ended.

As I gained more awareness of my emotions through the coaching, Willow held space for me to process them. Numbing out my emotions, especially anger, wasn't even something I was aware of I was doing. It wasn't helping me to numb out or stuff my emotions down. Willow gave me tools and methods for healthy ways to release anger and frustration. At the end of the coaching, I was not dependent on Willow as a coach - I know though if I needed her support with something I could contact her and she would be there for me.

I have and will continue to recommend friends and people looking for a transformational life coach to work with Willow. Because of Willow's passion and determination, she helped me to dissolve blocks that were holding me back. I stepped into a greater more empowered version of myself in not only my career but also in my relationships with others. Through the process of coaching with Willow, I feel more confident, happy and fulfilled in my life."

-Lizz C.

"I met Willow by divine intervention. She turned my life away from self-destruction with a slow turn towards self-construction. She has completely changed the way I deal with anxiety, hopelessness, Crazy imagination and fear. This book is packed with quotes and paragraphs suited to put you back on path, lift you up and help you move forward. I keep her book with me most of the time with Pages flagged to deal with my momentary relapses. One quick read and I am back on course. I have a long way to go and I am thankful Willow is my travel guide. God bless her and every soul she touches."

- Bill B

"First time I worked with Willow I didn't know what to think. Truly, she is straight-forward in manner and yet gentle. My session turned out to be an eye-opener in regards to getting right to the crux of what I was trying to put into words with her pointed questions and compassionate ear to hear what my heart was saying. She has a great way of finding out what matters most is so as to be able to help the client in the best way possible. The session for me was grounding, mind-blowing and surreal. Yet I left with the best intentions and renewed purpose and knowledge that Willow shifted my focus with higher good for me and the quick follow up before I left was like a mini powerhouse coaching tidbits to help me get started. I can't tell you how thankful I am to have worked with her and look forward to additional work in my future."

-Ann Marie "Nims" Meadows, Naples FL

ABOUT THE AUTHOR

I do not empower you. You have everything you need. I teach you how to tap into, harness and utilize the power that already exists within you.

Nourish wholeness, learn to access the solution from within.

Willow Green, Seeker and Sharer of Truth

Supporting your growth and expansion through her words, transformation sessions, and mentorship.

Willow believes true happiness is possible if we acknowledge, accept, and nourish all aspects of ourselves. Having completely turned her life around, she is an avid believer, model, and inspiration of how to transform negative thought patterns into opportunities and assets. She is guided by her inner compass and helping spirits

Willow has a tremendous sense of self-awareness from her personal journey through shadow self, addiction, energy blocks, self-love, and acceptance. She has a gift for turning tragedy to triumph. She personally overcame a drug addiction, eating disorder, and alcoholism. She has survived abuse, rape, and other physical trauma. She views all of these experiences as incredible gifts. Had she not been blessed with these experiences, she would not know how to help others heal from their own trauma. Willow lives every day in a state of gratitude for the ability to use her experiences to benefit others.

Willow's very unique and diverse set of credentials allow her tremendous success with clients both one-on-one and in small groups. Her ability to connect with her clients, right where they are and guide them to find their own truth is a gift. A gift she embraces from her personal journey through the fiery depths of darkness. Her goal is not to empower you, but to teach you how to connect to the power you already possess.

Willow's educational background includes an Occupational Science degree with focus on personal training, Certified Shamanic training through The Foundation For Shamanic Studies as well as a Shamanic, Herbalism Apprenticeship with Susun Weed. She owned a fitness club for 4 years. As a personal trainer, Willow's specialty has been working with Parkinson's Disease, post-stroke, and rehab clients for over 10 years. She learned the power of the mind and its effect on Dis-Ease as our thoughts, attitudes and beliefs truly create our reality. Working in the woods with Susun Weed, she learned how to create plant allies and connect with all of nature and its healing gifts. She has compiled her work and knowledge into a preventative maintenance program of removing the energy blocks that lead to Dis-Ease.

Willow is committed to holding space for others as they learn to love and nourish their whole self.

Willow Green

groovywillowgreen@gmail.com

Friend me on Facebook @groovywillowgreen

Please email me if you wish to set up your complimentary discovery call.

For more information on how you can work with me, I invite you to schedule a complimentary discovery call speak with me directly. Email GroovyWillowGreen@Gmail.com to set up your appointment.

Look for my next book

"Shattering the Illusion, Invoking True Love"

where I will take you on another journey. This journey will assist you in seeing through the illusions of fear. You will learn how to decipher the Truth and invoke True, healthy, love that lasts.

NOTES

Made in the USA
Middletown, DE
28 September 2018